■SCHOLASTIC

# ULTIMATE GUIDE TO
# BASEBALL

## By James Buckley, Jr.

**Produced by Shoreline Publishing Group LLC**

Santa Barbara, California

www.shorelinepublishing.com

President/Editorial Director: James Buckley, Jr.

Designed by Tom Carling, www.carlingdesign.com

Associate Editor: Jim Gigliotti

Index by Nanette Cardon, IRIS

Illustrations by Mike Arnold, www.arnomation.com

Photo Credits: Cover photo by Media 27. Interior photos courtesy of Focus on Baseball except the following: AP/Wide World: 30, 40, 41, 45, 65, 67, 69, 99, 118, 145, 151; Baseball Hall of Fame: 8, 9, 12, 19, 35, 39, 44, 63, 66, 68, 93, 123, 124, 125; Michael Burr: 32, 60, 61; Getty Images: 21, 29, 33 bottom, 38, 53, 56, 71, 75, 109, 135; Library of Congress: 14 (2), 140; Richmond (Virginia) Historical Society: 6

Thanks to Jackie Carter, Marie O'Neill, Elizabeth Ward, Janet Castiglione, Tim Daly, and Geoff Smith in the Scholastic Library Group for playing ball! Special thanks to Bill Pintard and the coaching staff of the Santa Barbara Foresters for their expertise.

Library of Congress Cataloging-in-Publication Data

Buckley, James.
  Ultimate guide to baseball / by James Buckley, Jr.
     p. cm. – (Scholastic ultimate guides)
  Includes bibliographical references and index.
  ISBN 978-0-531-20750-5 (alk. paper)
  1. Baseball–United States–History–Juvenile literature. I. Title.
  GV867.5.B855 2010
  796.357–dc22

                              2009043684

1 2 3 4 5 6 7 8 9 10 WCT 19 18 17 16 15 14 13 12 11 10

# INTRODUCTION

"Take me out to the ballgame, take me out with the crowd!" Well, that's what the song says (and they've been singing it since 1908!), but we hope you'll enjoy this awesome new book, the **Scholastic Ultimate Guide to Baseball**, in the comfort of your living room or library and not at the ballpark! After all, if you're too busy reading, you won't get a chance to snag that foul ball! (Then again, it's the perfect book for a rain delay!) But wherever you read it, this book covers "America's National Pastime" from the top of the first inning to the bottom of the ninth, from the first pitch to the final out.

We guarantee that your favorite team is in here . . . that's because we gave each team in Major League Baseball its own two-page section. You'll also find lots of other cool stuff, from tips on how to hit and pitch, to why a knuckleball isn't really a knuckleball. Plus, you'll meet heroes from Honus Wagner to Satchel Paige to Rickey Henderson to Albert Pujols.

Who knows? You might have so much fun with this book that you'll want to give away your tickets to the ballgame!

# CONTENTS

# PLAY BALL!

**It's our game,** America's game. It was born in fields and farms and grew to be a sport played by adults and kids in cities and towns. Baseball's early days were some of its most colorful, filled with memorable characters and amazing feats. In this chapter, we take a look at baseball in the late 1800s and early 1900s, when it was just a shadow of what it would become. Even then, however, it had already earned its most famous nickname: America's National Pastime.

## INSIDE:

*Richmond, Virginia, 1910: Rough-and-ready to play ball!*

# BEFORE BASEBALL

No one "invented" baseball. Instead, the game we know and love grew and changed over time. Historians have found evidence of all sorts of bat-and-ball games that people played in past centuries. There are even Egyptian hieroglyphs that show people throwing a ball and hitting a ball with a stick. Much, much later, British colonists brought their ball games to America. Settlers combined bits and pieces of these games, and by the 1830s the sport started to look like the game we play today. Here are three key moments from, as one author called it, "Baseball before we knew it."

## A Little Pretty Pocket-Book, 1744

This British book, reprinted in the American colonies, contains the first known mention of the word "base-ball." It includes this short poem:

> The ball once struck off,
> Away flies the boy
> To the next destined post
> And then home with joy.

## Town Law, Pittsfield, Mass., 1791

Historian John Thorn found a law from this small town that read, in part, "no person shall play baseball within 80 yards of the meeting house." They were worried about broken windows even way back then!

## The Boy's Own Book, 1834

This book contains a list of the rules of "Base, or Goal, Ball," a game that has a lot of similarities to today's baseball.

# SWING AND A
# MYTH

Let's get one thing straight, right off the, um . . . bat. Union Army General Abner Doubleday had as much to do with "inventing" baseball as you did. Lots of baseball books credit him as the game's inventor . . . and they're all wrong. The story of just how his name was connected to baseball's origin is a long and nasty one, but here's the short version. In 1905, a former player-turned-sporting-goods-magnate named Albert Spalding decided to "prove" that baseball had no British roots. He wanted to make sure that baseball was a purely American "invention."

Spalding put together a commission to investigate the issue. One piece of evidence was a letter from a guy named Abner Graves. Graves wrote that he was in Cooperstown, New York, in 1839 and watched Doubleday, not yet a general, lay out a baseball diamond and show some boys the game. The story was false. Wrong. Not true. Bogus. But Spalding had the "evidence" he wanted. He used the letter to "prove" that a good ol' American— and a man who was by then a Civil War hero—had invented baseball. The "Doubleday Myth" took firm hold and is the reason that the Hall of Fame is in Cooperstown today.

Your humble author asks that you do all in your power to erase this myth from existence. Thank you.

*I didn't invent baseball!*

# BASEBALL'S
# NEW YORK ROOTS

The Knickerbocker Club was founded in 1845 in New York City by, among others, a pair of sportsmen named Alexander Cartwright and Daniel "Doc" Adams. Together, these two men would do more to organize baseball than anyone before them.

When this club was founded, several other groups were already playing versions of what was often called "base ball," or just "ball." The Knickerbockers decided to create a list of rules that would straighten out the differences between the versions. Here are some rules from that list. Sound familiar?

## THE DIAMOND

"The bases shall be home to second base, 42 paces; and from first to third base, 42 paces."*

## FAIR OR FOUL?

"A ball knocked outside the range of the first or third base is foul."

## A DROPPED THIRD STRIKE

"Three balls being struck at and missed, and the last one caught, is a hand out; if not caught, is considered fair and the striker bound to run."

## END OF THE INNING

"Three hands out, all out."

## CATCHIN' FLIES

"A ball being struck or tipped and caught, either flying or on the first bound, is a hand out." **

## TAG, YOU'RE OUT!

"A player shall be out, if at any time when off a base he shall be touched by the ball in the hands of an adversary. . . . it being understood that in no instance is a ball to be thrown at him." ***

## GAME 1:
## A Riverside Rout

# A GAME OF BALL

**JUNE 19, 1846, HOBOKEN, NJ:** Upon the Elysian Field here, high above the foamy crests of the mighty Hudson, a game of "base ball" was played to the delight of dozens. Two teams from across the river met on the field of sporting battle to determine a victor in this new game of ball and bat. The New York Nine triumphed decisively by scoring 23 to the Knickerbocker Club's mere 1.

The defeat was galling for the sturdy Knickers, who have in recent days undertaken to lay out more rigid rules for the sport, which suffers from a want of organization. Your humble reporter is loathe to gaze upon his crystal ball and predict the future, but with a little help, this activity might find takers amid the sporting young men of our region.

*This meant that the distance between the bases was 30 yards, or 90 feet, just like today. **That's right—a catch on one bounce was an out; that rule was later changed. ***This was a big change; in many other "ball" games, striking a baserunner with a thrown ball was good for an out.

# GOIN' PRO

With baseball's popularity growing, someone had the bright idea to make money off the game. In 1862, William Cammeyer charged fans ten cents to watch games in Brooklyn, New York. To attract more customers, ballpark owners tried to get the best players. However, being a professional athlete was unheard of at the time. Athletes were supposed to compete only for love of the sport. But in 1869, the first pro baseball team, the Cincinnati Red Stockings, was formed. They did okay. They won all 57 games they played that season!

| PLAYER, POSITION | 1869 SALARY* |
|---|---|
| **Doug Allison,** Catcher | $800 |
| **Asa Brainard,** Pitcher | $1,100 |
| **Charlie Gould,** First Base | $800 |
| **Dick Hurley,** Substitute | $600 |
| **Andy Leonard,** Left Field | $800 |
| **Cal McVey,** Right Field | $800 |
| **Charlie Sweasy,** Second Base | $800 |
| **Fred Waterman,** Third Base | $1,000 |
| **George Wright,** Shortstop | $1,400 |
| **Harry Wright,** Center Field | $1,200 |

*Just for comparison, earning $1,000 in 1869 would be about the same as earning $232,000 today!

# BIRTH OF THE
# MAJORS

After a five-year run, the teams in the National Association (see page 14) needed some better organization. In 1876, they got it. Chicago owner William Hulbert put together owners of eight teams and created the National League of Professional Base Ball Clubs. The NL was the first "major league."

## 1876 NATIONAL LEAGUE TEAMS

**Boston Red Caps**

**Chicago White Stockings***

**Cincinnati Reds**

**Hartford Dark Blues**

**Louisville Grays**

**New York Mutuals**

**Philadelphia Athletics****

**St. Louis Brown Stockings**

*John Clarkson,*
*Chicago White Stockings*

* league champion; ** not the AL team; lasted only one year

In 1900, Ban Johnson, president of the minor's Western League, decided to compete with the mighty NL. Johnson renamed his league the American League and, in 1901, declared it a major league rival to the NL. After competing for players and fans for two years, the two leagues realized that they would be better off cooperating. In 1903, they agreed to stage a "World Series" between the champions of the two leagues at the end of every season.

## 1901 AMERICAN LEAGUE TEAMS

**Baltimore Orioles**

**Boston Americans**

**Chicago White Sox***

**Cleveland Blues**

**Detroit Tigers**

**Milwaukee Brewers**

**Philadelphia Athletics**

**Washington Senators**

*Cy Young,*
*Boston Americans*

* league champion

# OTHER LEAGUES

The National League was formed in 1876, but it was neither the first nor the last professional baseball league . . . It has just lasted the longest! Here's a quick look at some other pro baseball leagues.

## NATIONAL ASSOCIATION: 1871–1875

With the success of the Red Stockings, other pro teams were formed, and the NA was the first attempt at an organized pro league.

## AMERICAN ASSOCIATION: 1882–1891

The AA was formed after Cincinnati was kicked out of the NL for playing ball on Sundays and selling beer! The AA is also notable because it fielded the last African American major leaguer until Jackie Robinson in 1947—Moses "Fleetwood" Walker of the Toledo Blue Stockings.

## UNION ASSOCIATION: 1884

Nothing more than a one-year wonder.

## THE PLAYERS' LEAGUE: 1890

Players felt that team owners were cheating them out of money (and they were probably right). So the players tried to start their own teams. The experiment was short-lived.

## FEDERAL LEAGUE: 1914–1915

The last serious challenge to the majors came from a group of businessmen who were unable to buy AL or NL teams. They raided major league teams for players and even built some ballparks (such as Wrigley Field). But this league also flopped.

# EARLY STAR PLAYERS

Before the turn of the century (1900, that is), baseball produced a number of great players. Here are just a handful:

★ **Cap Anson** was the first player to reach 3,000 hits in his career. Playing for 27 years, mostly with the National League's Chicago team, and mostly at first base, he led the league in RBIs eight times.

★ In 1897, on his way to hitting .424, **Wee Willie Keeler** got a hit in 44 straight games, which is still the second-longest streak ever. He was famous for his batting advice, "Hit 'em where they ain't."

★ **James "King" Kelly** combined a winning personality with speed on the bases and a powerful bat. He was one of the most popular players of the era.

★ **John Ward** was the second pitcher to throw a perfect game. After hurting his arm, he moved to the outfield and then to the middle infield, where he continued to be one of the top "ballists." He helped form the Players' League in 1890. ▶▶▶

★ **George Wright** was the first great baseball superstar. In fact, in 1937, he was elected to the Baseball Hall of Fame. He was an outstanding cricket player who easily switched to baseball.

★ **Harry Wright** was a good player, but was much better as a manager and organizer. He joined his brother George in the Hall in 1953 for helping to form the Red Stockings.

# DEFUNCT TEAMS

More than 60 teams have come and gone from the "major leagues." However, all but a few of them came and went before 1900. Here's a list of some of the teams that stuck around for more than a year or two. (Among the one-year wonders: Baltimore Monumentals, Cincinnati Kelly's Killers, Cleveland Infants, and Wilmington Quicksteps.)

## Baltimore Orioles*
1882–1899

## Buffalo Bisons
1879–1885

## Cleveland Spiders
1887–1899

## Detroit Wolverines
1881–1888

## Louisville Colonels
1882–1899

## Providence Grays
1878–1885

## Troy Trojans
1879–1882

## Worcester Ruby Legs
1880–1882

## SQUASHED SPIDERS

The Cleveland Spiders' final season was one for the record books—the *bottom* of the record books. The Spiders managed to win only 20 of their 154 games. Their single-season record of 134 losses should be safe for quite a while!

*Today's Orioles took their name from this older team.

# EARLY RULES
# ODDITIES

Remember how some of the first rules of baseball were pretty much the same as today's (see page 10)? Well, some of the rules were very different! Here's a look at some rules from baseball's early years that might surprise today's players and fans.

☑ A batted ball caught after one bounce was an out (until 1864).

☑ Until 1887, a batter could indicate whether he wanted the pitch to be above the waist or below. If the pitcher threw it right over the plate, but not at the requested height . . . it was called a ball!

☑ Four balls equal a walk, right? Well, not at first. It took nine balls to earn a walk in the 1860s. That changed to five balls in 1887 and finally to four balls in 1889.

☑ A great overhand curve? Not legal until 1884. Until then, pitchers had to throw under-handed or sidearm. ▶▶▶

☑ There was no pitcher's mound. The pitcher stood in a square in the dirt that was only 50 feet from home plate! The distance was changed to 60 feet six inches in 1894.

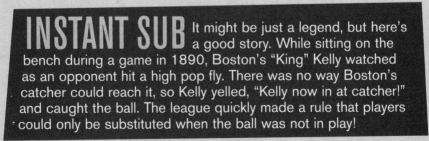

## INSTANT SUB
It might be just a legend, but here's a good story. While sitting on the bench during a game in 1890, Boston's "King" Kelly watched as an opponent hit a high pop fly. There was no way Boston's catcher could reach it, so Kelly yelled, "Kelly now in at catcher!" and caught the ball. The league quickly made a rule that players could only be substituted when the ball was not in play!

# TALKIN' BASEBALL: 1902

If you could go back in time to the early 20th century, the game of baseball would look familiar. But you might not understand what the players were saying. Baseball has always had its own wonderful language (and there are lots of examples of it in this book). But in its early days, players used expressions that would have today's players scratching their batting helmets in confusion. Here are a few examples. See whether you can figure out what they mean before you read the translations.

### "The ballist tried to break up some great box-work with a baby act."

**TRANSLATION:** The batter tried to bunt for a hit against a really good pitcher.

**"If we soak enough batsmen, we'll have a chance at the gonfalon!"**

TRANSLATION: If we retire enough batters, we might win the pennant!

**"If these muffins can't tally in this inning, we'll be looking at a whitewash!"**

TRANSLATION: If these young players can't score this inning, we'll get shut out.

**"The cranks were really chaffing that ballist, who was an ice wagon on the base paths."**

TRANSLATION: The fans were really making fun of the player, who was a very slow runner.

**"After we take this pianola, we'll be lugging the bunting!"**

TRANSLATION: After we win this easy game, we'll take home the pennant!

# HERO TIME

### HONUS WAGNER, Shortstop
#### Louisville: 1897–1899; Pittsburgh: 1900–1917
Although Wagner played his last game more than 90 years ago, he remains one of the top dozen all-around players ever. Wagner was an eight-time NL batting champion and a terrific fielder, and he once held the record for steals in a career. When the Hall of Fame was founded in 1936, Wagner was elected one of its first five members.

### TY COBB, Outfield ▶▶▶
#### Detroit: 1905–1926; Philadelphia Athletics: 1927–1928
Cobb was disliked by nearly everyone for his nasty personality. But even his enemies agreed that he was an almost perfect baseball player. His .366 career average (he won 11 batting titles) is still the best ever. When he retired, he was the all-time leader in hits, runs, and steals. Cobb did anything he could, legal or otherwise, to win.

# BALTIMORE ORIOLES

One of the AL's oldest teams, Baltimore has not been one of its best lately. However, the Orioles have a great ballpark, some good young players, and loyal fans. Who knows? Maybe the O's can rack up some W's soon!

## GAME 1?
## 1901

The team that is now the Orioles started in Milwaukee and moved to St. Louis in 1902. In 1954, the St. Louis Browns moved east and became the Baltimore Orioles.

 ## MAGIC MOMENT
### Cal's Good Streak

In 1995, Cal Ripken Jr. broke Lou Gehrig's record by playing in his 2,131st straight game. Rip would retire with 2,632 straight.

 ## LOWEST LOW
### O's Bad Streak

Talk about getting off on the wrong foot! In 1998, the Orioles set a record by losing their first 21 games!

## STUFF

HOME:
**Oriole Park at Camden Yards**

WORLD SERIES TITLES: **3**

ONLY IN BALTIMORE:
**Former O's slugger Boog Powell can often be seen dishing up BBQ at his restaurant behind center field.**

## STAR SEASONS!

**1966** After 65 seasons of futility, the Orioles finally won a World Series championship.

**1970** Third baseman Brooks Robinson made some amazing defensive plays to help Baltimore win another Series.

**1983** Led by MVP Cal Ripken Jr., the Orioles knocked off the Philadelphia Phillies to win their third World Series.

## The Ultimate Oriole
# CAL RIPKEN JR.

Ripken is best known for his consecutive-games-played streak of 2,632, but he also helped change how we think of shortstops. "Rip" was the first tall shortstop (6'3") to succeed as a batter and fielder. He was also the 1983 AL MVP and a 19-time All-Star. He entered the Hall of Fame in 2007.

**#1**

# FUNKY FACTS

➜ In 1954, the Orioles took their name from a team of the same name from the 1890s. Those Orioles won three Temple Cups, an early version of the World Series.

➜ One of the Orioles' most famous fans was "Wild Bill" Hagy. He used to stand on top of the dugout and spell out "O-R-I-O-L-E-S" with his body while fans chanted the letters.

➜ The 1971 Orioles were the last big-league team to have four pitchers each win at least 20 games. Mike Cuellar, Pat Dobson, and Jim Palmer won 20, while Dave McNally got 21.

## SUPERSTAR! NICK MARKAKIS

This young outfielder is one of the players the team hopes to build on in the future. A .300 hitter with one of the best throwing arms in baseball, Markakis also has base-stealing speed.

➜ Orioles manager Earl Weaver led the team to four World Series. He loved to argue with umps. He was once thrown out of *both* games of a doubleheader.

**You Can Look It Up!** THE O's OFFICIAL WEBSITE: www.baltimoreorioles.com

# BOSTON
# RED SOX

Fans in the "Red Sox Nation" were thrilled when their team finally won a World Series in 2004 after an 86-year drought. The Sox are among the most beloved teams in the majors, with fans all across the (American) nation.

## GAME 1?
## 1901

The Boston Americans joined the AL in 1901, its first year as a major league. They were renamed the Red Sox in 1908. Until World War I, they were one of the AL's best.

 ## MAGIC MOMENT
### 2004 World Series

Finally! Whew! That took a while! After 86 years, the Red Sox won a World Series! They also beat the hated Yankees in the ALCS.

 ## LOWEST LOW
### The Curse Begins

In 1920, the Red Sox sold a young lefty pitcher with a little power to the Yankees. So what? So he turned into Babe Ruth!

## STUFF

**HOME:**
**Fenway Park**

WORLD SERIES TITLES: **5**

ONLY IN BOSTON:
**Fenway's left-field wall is known as the Green Monster (um, 'cause it's green). It's 37 feet tall, just 310 feet from home plate.**

## STAR SEASONS!

**1918** With Ruth setting pitching records, Boston won its third Series in four years . . . and its last until 2004.

**1941** Superstar Ted Williams finished with a .406 batting average. No one has topped Williams—or .400—since.

**2007** Led by Manny Ramirez and David Ortiz, the Red Sox won another World Series.

## The Ultimate Red Sox
# TED WILLIAMS

He grew up wanting to be "the greatest hitter who ever lived." Many experts think he made his dream come true. A .344 career hitter, he also had 521 homers. He did all that even while missing parts of five seasons to serve as a military pilot. "Teddy Ballgame," the "Splendid Splinter," was one of the best.

**#1**

# FUNKY FACTS

➔ When Fenway Park was first built in 1912, there was a dirt mound at the bottom of the left-field wall. Outfielder Hugh Duffy had to run up the mound so often to chase fly balls that it was called "Duffy's Cliff."

➔ From 1941 through 1988, the Red Sox had only three regular left fielders, and all of them are in the Hall of Fame. Ted Williams (1939–1960), Carl "Yaz" Yastrzemski (1961–1983), and Jim Rice (1974–1989) formed that amazing trio.

➔ The Red Sox do have a mascot, but to be honest, most fans don't pay much attention to him. He's a big green monster-like thing known as "Wally," after Fenway's left-field wall.

## SUPERSTAR!
# DUSTIN PEDROIA

Pedroia is the definition of "scrappy." He's small, but he doesn't let that stop him. He was the AL MVP in 2008 and helped the Sox win the '07 Series. The second baseman always ends the game dirty.

➔ Since 2003, Red Sox fans have been able to sit on top of the Green Monster. Three rows of seats atop the left-field wall give fans a Monster's-eye view of the action.

**You Can Look It Up!** BOSTON'S OFFICIAL WEBSITE: www.redsox.com

# NEW YORK YANKEES

The numbers say it all: 27 World Series titles, more than any other team. In fact, that's more championships than any team in major American sports! No matter what era or decade, the Yanks have always been among the best.

## GAME 1?
## 1901

Today's Yanks started as an early version of the Baltimore Orioles. They moved to New York in 1903 and were called the Highlanders until they got their current name in 1913.

 ## MAGIC MOMENT
### 1923 World Series

Every dynasty starts somewhere, and this is where the Yanks' did. Thanks to Babe Ruth, New York won it all for the first time.

 ## LOWEST LOW
### 1966: Yuck

It's hard to find a low for this team, but let's go with 1966, when the Yankees finished last for the first time since 1912.

## STUFF

**HOME:**
**Yankee Stadium**

**WORLD SERIES TITLES: 27**

**ONLY IN NEW YORK:**
**Before every game, fans can visit Monument Park to see plaques and statues honoring Yankee greats.**

## STAR SEASONS!

**1927** Was this the greatest team ever? Some experts think so. They won the AL by 19 games and swept the Series.

**1953** The Yankees topped even themselves this season when they won their record fifth straight World Series.

**2009** The Yanks won their first Series since 2000, beating the defending-champion Phillies.

## The Ultimate Yankee
# LOU GEHRIG

Not only was Gehrig one of the greatest hitters of all time (13 seasons with 100 RBIs! 23 grand slams! AL-record 184 RBIs in 1931!), he was also one of the bravest. He played 2,130 straight games, ignoring a variety of injuries. Sadly, he had to retire because of a nerve disease that took his life in 1941.

# FUNKY FACTS

➜ Most pitchers these days don't finish what they start. It wasn't always that way. In 1904, Yanks pitcher Jack Chesbro completed 48 starts in a row! The 2009 MLB leader had nine!

➜ In 1929, the Yankees became the first team to regularly use numbers on their team jerseys. The numbers were assigned by batting order, so Babe Ruth was No. 3 and Lou Gehrig was No. 4.

➜ Speaking of numbers, the Yankees have retired 15 of them, more than any other team. In fact, there are only two single-digit numbers left. Derek Jeter's No. 2 figures to be retired one day, along with former manager Joe Torre's No. 6.

## SUPERSTAR!
# ALEX RODRIGUEZ

A-Rod can flat-out mash. He is one of only four players in the last 40 years to win batting, RBI, and home-run crowns. He joined the Yanks in 2004 and has since won two of his three MVP awards.

➜ The Yankees even had a famous stadium announcer. Bob Sheppard was at the mic from 1951 to 2007. Derek Jeter insists on being announced by a recording of Sheppard instead of by the current announcer.

**You Can Look It Up!** NEW YORK'S OFFICIAL WEBSITE: www.yankees.com

# TAMPA BAY RAYS

The newest member of the AL, the Rays were the "least of the East" for nine out of their first ten seasons. Then in 2008, they earned their first playoff berth—and won the AL pennant. This is a young team with a bright future!

## GAME 1? 1998

After blocking the San Francisco Giants' move to Florida, Major League Baseball gave an expansion team to Tampa. The team was called the Devil Rays until 2008.

 ## MAGIC MOMENT
### 2008 ALCS

After whomping the White Sox in the division series, the Rays beat the Red Sox to win the team's first AL championship.

 ## LOWEST LOW
### Pick One

Expansion teams often struggle to become good, but sheesh! Tampa lost 90 or more games for ten straight years!

## STUFF

**HOME:**
**Tropicana Field**

**WORLD SERIES TITLES: 0**

**ONLY IN TAMPA:**
**Fans at Tropicana Field can touch real, live rays in a 35-foot, 10,000-gallon tank located beyond the outfield wall.**

## STAR SEASONS!

**2003** Outfielder Carl Crawford led the AL with 55 stolen bases, the first of four times he would do so.

**2004** For the first time, Tampa didn't finish last in the AL East. It finished fourth out of five!

**2008** Thanks to his 27 homers and great defense at third, Evan Longoria was named AL Rookie of the Year.

# CARL CRAWFORD

The speedy outfielder has spent his whole career with Tampa. He muddled through the down years until the squad emerged big-time in 2008. A three-time league leader in triples, he is one of the most exciting players in the game. His home-run-robbing catch earned him the 2009 All-Star Game MVP award.

**#1**

# FUNKY FACTS

→ The Rays were featured in a very popular baseball movie. *The Rookie* told the story of pitcher Jim Morris, who made the 1999 Rays after spending many years as a high school baseball coach.

→ Doesn't anyone want to play here? Business leaders in Tampa tried to lure the White Sox, Mariners, and Giants to the area. None ended up coming, but baseball finally gave the city an expansion team.

→ One of the most famous players to grow up in Tampa ended his Hall of Fame career as a Ray. Wade Boggs, who won five AL batting titles with Boston, joined Tampa Bay in 1999. With the

## SUPERSTAR! EVAN LONGORIA

After only two seasons in the bigs, Longoria is regarded as one of the best in the game. In a 2009 poll, fellow players named him most likely to make the Hall of Fame. He's a great defender with a power bat.

Rays, he got his 3,000th career hit . . . and it was a homer!

→ Big-league teams have held their spring training near Tampa since 1922.

**You Can Look It Up!** TAMPA BAY'S OFFICIAL WEBSITE: www.raysbaseball.com

# TORONTO
# BLUE JAYS

The Blue Jays are the only Canadian team in Major League Baseball (the Montreal Expos moved to Washington, D.C., in 2005). The Jays are also the only non-U.S. team to win the World Series!

## GAME 1?
## 1977

With Montreal in the NL, the AL got its own team north of the border when the Blue Jays were awarded to Toronto. The team took its name from a newspaper contest.

 ## MAGIC MOMENT
### Carter's Blast

Joe Carter became only the second player ever to win a World Series with a homer. His ended Game 6 and the Series in 1993.

 ## LOWEST LOW
### Very "Blue" Jays

After the Jays lost a team-record 109 games in 1979, Canadian fans were wondering whether they could return the team.

## STUFF

HOME:
**Rogers Centre**

WORLD SERIES TITLES: 2

ONLY IN TORONTO:
**A hotel inside the stadium—which was once called the SkyDome—has rooms with views of the playing field!**

## STAR SEASONS!

**1987** Outfielder George Bell won the AL MVP award, with 47 homers and a league-leading 134 RBIs.

**1992** The Blue Jays became the first Canadian team to win a World Series, defeating the Braves in six games.

**2003** Ace pitcher Roy "Doc" Halladay won the AL Cy Young Award, going 22–7.

## The Ultimate Blue Jay
# DAVE STIEB

He has some competition from players such as George Bell and Tony Fernandez, but with 15 seasons (1979–1992, 1998) on the mound in Toronto, Dave Stieb is our *Ultimate* Jay. He's the team's career leader in wins, innings pitched, and strikeouts. He was a seven-time All-Star and won at least 16 games six different seasons.

**#1**

# FUNKY FACTS

➜ Toronto's Rogers Centre is the only major league ballpark where "The Star-Spangled Banner" is not played last before a game. They play "O Canada," of course!

➜ The Blue Jays pulled off a rare feat by winning three straight Cy Young awards. Pat Hentgen won it in 1996, and then Roger Clemens won back-to-back awards in 1997–1998.

➜ In 2003, first baseman Carlos Delgado accomplished one of baseball's rarest hitting feats. The slugger whacked four homers in one game, becoming only the 13th player to do so.

➜ The Blue Jays won a 1977 game against the Orioles by

## SUPERSTAR!
# AARON HILL

*A solid second baseman, Hill emerged in 2009 as one of the key players in Toronto's offense. He was among AL leaders in hits, total bases, and at-bats. Plus, he made his first All-Star team.*

forfeit. Baltimore manager Earl Weaver pulled his team from the field in the fifth inning, claiming a tarp in the bullpen created a hazard. Toronto's Jim Clancy just happened to be working on a two-hit, 4–0 shutout at the time!

**You Can Look It Up!** TORONTO'S OFFICIAL WEBSITE: www.bluejays.com

# HITTING!

**What's the most fun part** of baseball? Hitting, of course! In this chapter, we'll take an inside look at the bats and the men who wield them. Batting is certainly one of the hardest jobs in sports, but even if all you can do is watch the best, it's still a thrill to see a fastball turn into a home run in a split second. So get ready to swing the stick, hit the pill, shoot the gap, smack a seeing-eye single, or lay down a perfect suicide squeeze. And if you don't know what all that means, you will . . . in about 14 pages!

## INSIDE:

*Today's fans enjoy one of the best hitters ever: Albert Pujols.*

# HOW TO MAKE A BAT

Bats actually do grow on trees. Okay, they grow *in* trees. Here are the six steps that a bat goes through before it's ready to be used in a game.

**SPLIT:** a chunk of wood with the bark attached

**SQUARE:** the split is sawed into a rectangular shape

**ROUND:** the edges are cut off and smoothed

**ROUGH CUT:** carved on a lathe, it now looks like a bat

**SEMI-FINISHED:** sanded and smoothed, it's nearly done

**FINISHED:** stained and polished . . . time to hit!

## Inside the Baseball

You've got a bat . . . now you need something to hit. Here are the layers of material inside a major league baseball, starting from the center and working outward:

Cork and rubber center "pill" > Layer of black rubber > Layer of red rubber > 4-ply cotton winding (like yarn) > 3-ply white wool winding > 4-ply gray winding > Cotton finish winding > White-tanned cowhide leather > Hand-sewn with waxed, red cotton thread

# HOW TO GET
# A HIT

Hitting a round, speeding, spinning baseball with a round, wood bat has been called one of the most—if not *the* most—difficult tasks in sports. It must be hard if a hitter who only fails seven out of ten times is considered really good! These photos show a great batting stance and a great swing. Our notes explain some of the key parts of each.

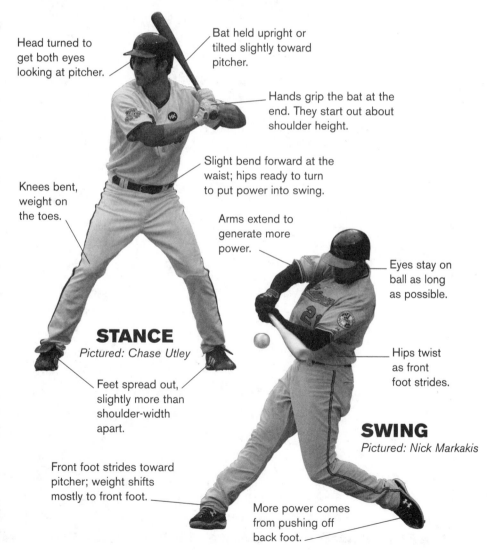

Head turned to get both eyes looking at pitcher.

Bat held upright or tilted slightly toward pitcher.

Hands grip the bat at the end. They start out about shoulder height.

Slight bend forward at the waist; hips ready to turn to put power into swing.

Knees bent, weight on the toes.

Arms extend to generate more power.

Eyes stay on ball as long as possible.

## STANCE
*Pictured: Chase Utley*

Feet spread out, slightly more than shoulder-width apart.

Hips twist as front foot strides.

## SWING
*Pictured: Nick Markakis*

Front foot strides toward pitcher; weight shifts mostly to front foot.

More power comes from pushing off back foot.

# FIGURING HITTING

Baseball loooooves statistics. It's a math geek's favorite sport! But stats aren't just for geeks: Regular fans should be able to use them, too. Here are the formulas you'll need to check out your own performance at the plate!

## BATTING AVERAGE (BA)

$$H \div AB = BA$$

Number of hits (H) divided by number of official at-bats (AB)

Example: 125 H $\div$ 428 AB = .292 BA

Remember, you don't count a walk, a sacrifice, or a hit by pitch as an official at-bat.

## SLUGGING PERCENTAGE (SLG)

$$TB \div AB = SLG$$

Number of total bases (TB: a single is 1 base, a double is 2 bases, etc.) divided by number of official at-bats

Example: 78 singles + 26 doubles + 4 triples + 17 home runs = 210 total bases

210 TB $\div$ 428 AB = .491 SLG

## ON-BASE PERCENTAGE (OBP)

$$(H + BB + HBP) \div (AB + BB + HBP + SAC) = OBP$$

Number of times reaching base divided by number of total times at bat

Example: (125 H + 28 BB* + 5 HBP**) $\div$ (428 official AB + 28 BB + 5 HBP + 1 sacrifice bunt) = .342

OBP, unlike batting average, measures walks as well as hits. When you're trying to score, all that matters is that you get on base!

*base on balls; **hit by pitch

# TOP FIVES

Here's a quick primer on the best of all time in three key statistical batting categories. Hall of Famers galore!

## CAREER BATTING AVERAGE

| | |
|---|---|
| Ty COBB | .366 |
| Rogers HORNSBY | .359 |
| Joe JACKSON | .356 |
| Lefty O'DOUL | .349 |
| Ed DELAHANTY | .346 |

## CAREER SLUGGING PERCENTAGE

| | |
|---|---|
| Babe RUTH | .690 |
| Ted WILLIAMS | .634 |
| Lou GEHRIG | .632 |
| Albert PUJOLS* | .628 |
| Jimmie FOXX | .609 |

## CAREER ON-BASE PERCENTAGE

| | |
|---|---|
| Ted WILLIAMS | .482 |
| Babe RUTH | .474 |
| Lou GEHRIG | .447 |
| Barry BONDS | .444 |
| Rogers HORNSBY | .434 |

*active player in 2009

# HOW TO

Once you step up to the plate (and we'll say you're batting with one out and a runner on first base to make things easier), we count 11 ways that you can make it on base. Here's our list. But before you read the page, see how many you can come up with on your own!

## 1. Single

## 2. Double

## 3. Triple

## 4. Home Run

Although you don't stay on base, this counts as having made it onto the bases. And an inside-the-park home run counts here, too!

## 5. Walk

## 6. Intentional Walk

## 7. Error

## 8. Hit by Pitch

## 9. Dropped Third Strike

If you swing and miss at a third strike and the catcher doesn't make a clean catch, you can run to first. If the catcher doesn't tag you or throw to first before you get there, you are safe!

# GET ON BASE

## 10. Fielder's Choice

That's when you hit a ball that results in one of your teammates being put out on the bases, but you reach base yourself. You are charged with an at-bat, but you don't get credit for a hit.

## 11. Catcher's Interference

This usually happens if you hit the catcher's mitt during a swing. If the ump sees that, the swing is not counted and you are awarded first base.

# HOMER TIME!

Whether you call it a long ball, a shot, a dinger, a tater . . . whether you "kiss it good-bye!" or "watch it leave the yard" or just shout, "Holy cow!" a home run is baseball's big play. For batters, it's the best you can do: Hit it out of the park and score for your team. For fielders and pitchers, it's the ultimate frustration. You have to just stand there and watch. Here are some lists of home-run superstars.

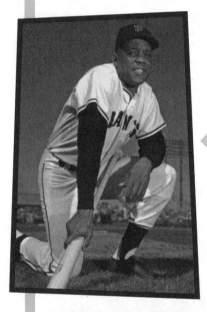

## CAREER LEADERS

| PLAYER | HOME RUNS |
|---|---|
| Barry **BONDS** | 762 |
| Hank **AARON** | 755 |
| Babe **RUTH** | 714 |
| Willie **MAYS** | 660 |
| Ken **GRIFFEY JR.*** | 630 |
| Sammy **SOSA** | 609 |
| Frank **ROBINSON** | 586 |
| Mark **McGWIRE** | 583 |
| Alex **RODRIGUEZ*** | 583 |
| Harmon **KILLEBREW** | 573 |

*active player in 2009

## The Steroid Issue

No discussion of home runs can be honest without a note about steroids and other "performance-enhancing" drugs (PEDs). In the 1990s, it became apparent that some players were taking drugs that helped them become very strong very quickly. Although these drugs had been banned by Major League Baseball, little was done to stop players from taking them. As a result, many records set in the 1990s and 2000s are now questionable. Were players breaking records because of their skills, or by cheating? A handful of players, some of them famous, have tested positive for PEDs since testing began in 2003. However, no players have had their records taken away ... yet.

## Four in One Game!

Hitting four homers in one game is one of the rarest feats in baseball. Here's the complete list since 1900:

| PLAYER, TEAM | YEAR |
|---|---|
| Lou **GEHRIG**, Yankees | 1932 |
| Chuck **KLEIN**, Phillies | 1936 |
| Pat **SEEREY**, White Sox | 1948 |
| Gil **HODGES**, Dodgers | 1950 |
| Joe **ADCOCK**, Braves | 1954 |
| Rocky **COLAVITO**, Indians | 1959 |
| Willie **MAYS**, Giants | 1961 |
| Mike **SCHMIDT**, Phillies | 1976 |
| Bob **HORNER**, Braves | 1986 |
| Mark **WHITEN**, Cardinals | 1993 |
| Mike **CAMERON**, Mariners | 2002 |
| Shawn **GREEN**, Dodgers | 2003 |
| Carlos **DELGADO**, Blue Jays | 2003 |

# SINGLE-SEASON LEADERS

| PLAYER, TEAM | TOTAL | YEAR |
|---|---|---|
| Barry **BONDS**, Giants | **73** | 2001 |
| Mark **McGWIRE**, Cardinals | **70** | 1998 |
| Sammy **SOSA**, Cubs | **66** | 1998 |
| Mark **McGWIRE**, Cardinals | **65** | 1999 |
| Sammy **SOSA**, Cubs | **64** | 2001 |
| Sammy **SOSA**, Cubs | **63** | 1999 |
| Roger **MARIS**, Yankees | **61** | 1961 |
| Babe **RUTH**, Yankees | **60** | 1927 |
| Babe **RUTH**, Yankees | **59** | 1921 |
| Jimmie **FOXX**, Athletics | **58** | 1932 |
| Hank **GREENBERG**, Tigers | **58** | 1938 |
| Ryan **HOWARD**, Phillies | **58** | 2006 |
| Mark **McGWIRE**, Athletics/Cardinals | **58** | 1997 |

# THE TRIPLE CROWN

Here's a trivia question for you: What has not been done since 1967 . . . and not in the NL since 1937? It's among the most difficult hitting feats: the Triple Crown. It happens when a player leads his league in home runs, runs batted in, and batting average in a season. To win a Triple Crown, a player must combine power, plate discipline, and the ability to produce in the clutch.

| PLAYER, TEAM | YEAR |
|---|---|
| **Carl Yastrzemski**, Red Sox | 1967 |
| **Frank Robinson**, Orioles | 1966 |
| **Mickey Mantle**, Yankees | 1956 |
| **Ted Williams**, Red Sox | 1947 |
| **Ted Williams**, Red Sox | 1942 |
| **Joe Medwick**, Cardinals | 1937 |
| **Lou Gehrig**, Yankees | 1934 |
| **Jimmie Foxx**, Athletics | 1933 |
| **Chuck Klein**, Phillies | 1933 |
| **Rogers Hornsby**, Cardinals | 1925 |
| **Rogers Hornsby**, Cardinals | 1922 |
| **Ty Cobb**, Tigers | 1909 |
| **Nap Lajoie**, Athletics | 1901 |

## TRIPLE CROWN CAREERS

Since 1967, when "Yaz" (right) won baseball's last Triple Crown, a trio of superstars and one pretty darned good player have each earned a league title in all three categories—just not all in the same season. Can you name these four players?

ANSWER: Barry Bonds, Manny Ramirez, Alex Rodríguez . . . and Andres Galarraga!

# DETAILS OF
# THE BUNT

We celebrate superstar, all-around sluggers on the opposite page. Here, we take a time out to look at baseball's littlest hits: bunts. Bunts don't make the fans leap to their feet like soaring home runs or clutch doubles, but players know how important bunts can be to winning. Here are some facts about bunting.

**HOW TO BUNT** Turn your body so that your shoulders and face are square to the pitcher. Slide your top hand up the bat to just below the bat's fattest point. Keep the head of the bat angled upward. Keep your fingers behind the bat! As the pitch hits the bat, let it give just a little. You can angle the bat to direct the ball toward one foul line or the other.

**SACRIFICE BUNT** This type of bunt is made to let a baserunner advance; the idea is to bunt so that the fielders can only throw you out and not throw out the lead runner.

**BUNT FOR A HIT** Speedy runners can try to reach base with a drag bunt—running out of the batter's box at the same time as they bunt. Then it's a race for first.

**SQUEEZE BUNTS** A squeeze bunt is used with a runner on third. A safety squeeze is when the runner takes off for home once he sees that the bunt has been made. A suicide squeeze is when the runner takes off with the pitch . . . and the batter has to get the bunt down or the runner is toast!

## Bunt Facts

**Most Bunt Hits in a Season** (since 1974)
★ **Brett Butler**, Dodgers: **42** in 1992 ▶▶▶

**Most Sacrifices in a Career**
★ **Eddie Collins**, A's/White Sox: **512***

**Most Sacrifices in a Season**
★ **Ray Chapman**, Indians: **67*** in 1917

*includes sacrifice bunts and sacrifice flies

# TALKIN' BASEBALL: 2010

We've already seen baseball language from about 100 years ago (page 18). How does the sport sound today? New words and phrases enter baseball all the time. *The Dickson Baseball Dictionary* runs more than 1,000 pages! Use your inside baseball knowledge and see whether you can translate some sentences that you might hear at today's ballparks.

## "He brought me the cheese, but I took him yard!"

**TRANSLATION:** He threw me a great fastball, but I hit it for a home run!

## "With a splitter and his Uncle Charlie, that guy has filthy stuff!"

**TRANSLATION:** With a great split-fingered fastball and curveball, that pitcher has two pitches that are very hard to hit!

## "Gordon is up with ducks on the pond; this would be a good spot for a gapper."

**TRANSLATION:** Gordon is up with the bases loaded; this would be a good time for him to hit a line drive into the gap between two outfielders.

## "He was in an 0-2 hole, but then he hit an oppo at-em ball right on the screws."

**TRANSLATION:** The batter had two strikes and no balls, but then he hit a hard, opposite-field line drive that unfortunately went directly to a fielder for an out.

▲ "After he watched it go down the pipe, he got rung up. He was frozen pizza!"

**TRANSLATION:** After the batter watched a fastball go right down the middle of the plate, the umpire called him out on strikes. The batter was standing there as if he were frozen!

"They said this scrubeenie was a masher, but all I see is a banjo hitter."

**TRANSLATION:** They said this young player could really hit the ball hard and far, but all I see is a light hitter.

"The hot corner got a candy hop, and then it was around the horn for the DP."

**TRANSLATION:** The third baseman fielded a ground ball that came to him on an easy bounce, and then he threw to second base to start a double play.

# HERO TIME

## Babe Ruth

**Babe Ruth hit** his last homer before baseball was on TV, before World War II, and before Alaska and Hawaii were states! And yet all these years later, he is still regarded as the finest baseball player of all time.

A Baltimore schoolboy star, Ruth joined the Boston Red Sox in 1914. By 1916, he was a top pitcher in the majors. That's right, Ruth was a pitcher. He helped the Red Sox win two World Series and set a record for shutout innings in the Series that stood for 43 years! He also started playing outfield, and set a new record in 1919 with 29 homers. He wasn't done yet.

Moving to the Yankees in 1920, he slugged 54 homers, more than every other *team* in the league! He hit 59 in 1921 and then stunned the sports world with 60 in 1927! He and the Yankees dominated baseball in the 1920s and 1930s, with Ruth winning a total of 12 home-run titles. He also led the league in runs eight times, RBIs six times, and walks 11 times.

Ruth put together a stunning .690 career slugging percentage, still the highest of all time. And he whacked 714 home runs. Until Hank Aaron topped him in 1974, Ruth was the king.

He was a gigantic personality, a big man with big appetites. In a time when America was struggling with the Great Depression, Ruth was the Great Success.

# Jackie Robinson

**Sometimes athletes** move from the sports world to the wider national stage. They go beyond ballparks and games and make their mark on society. On that short list of people, one name stands above the rest: Jackie Robinson.

A multi-talented athlete in college, Robinson was playing baseball in the Negro Leagues when he got a call that would change his life ... and America. Branch Rickey of the Brooklyn Dodgers asked Robinson to become the first African American player in the modern major leagues. For decades, baseball owners had agreed not to hire black players, but Rickey thought that was wrong.

Robinson knew that he faced many challenges. Racist fans would hate him, bigoted players would try to hurt him. Would his teammates accept him? He stuck with it and, in 1947, made his debut in Brooklyn. Over the next decade, he became both an inspiration for the civil rights movement and one of the game's great players. His speed and daring on the base paths were legendary.

Robinson's courage in breaking the "color line," as it was called, made him a hero. In 1997, 50 years after his breakthrough, Major League Baseball retired his No. 42 jersey ... for all teams and for all time.

# CHICAGO
# WHITE SOX

Although they've had a bit more success than the nationally popular Cubs, the White Sox are seen as Chicago's "second" team. But unlike the Cubs, at least the White Sox can say that they've won a World Series since 1908!

## GAME 1?
## 1901

The AL was formed in 1901 by Ban Johnson, who owned the White Sox. He made his team the centerpiece of the new league, which challenged the older NL for players and fans.

 ## MAGIC MOMENT
### 2005 World Series

Finally ridding themselves of the "Black Sox" curse, the White Sox beat the Houston Astros in four straight games.

## LOWEST LOW
### 1919 World Series

The White Sox were dubbed the "Black Sox" after some players took money from gamblers to lose the Series on purpose.

## STUFF

HOME:
**U.S. Cellular Field**

WORLD SERIES TITLES: **3**

ONLY IN CHICAGO:
**Fans can cool off on hot Chicago afternoons by taking a quick spin in the large shower behind the center-field wall.**

## STAR SEASONS!

**1906** The "Hitless Wonders" (team average: .230) had enough pitching to win the Sox's first World Series.

**1959** For the first time since the Black Sox scandal of 1919, the White Sox won the AL.

**1994** Frank Thomas won his second straight AL MVP award in a season that was shortened by a labor dispute.

## The Ultimate White Sox

# FRANK THOMAS

Playing in Chicago from 1990–2005, Thomas became the White Sox's all-time leader in just about every major batting category. Thomas was known as "The Big Hurt" for what he did to the baseball and his opponents. A ten-time .300 hitter, he had a rare combination of power and batting eye.

**#1**

# FUNKY FACTS

➔ The 1959 White Sox were a young team that used speed on the bases to win the AL title. Their hustle inspired fans to nickname them the "Go-Go Sox."

➔ One-time White Sox owner Bill Veeck was famous for trying anything to get fans to come to the park. In 1975, he tried out a new look for his team. He made players wear softball-style short pants. It was a flop. The players hated them, and the experiment only lasted one game!

➔ Another Veeck idea was even more unsuccessful. In 1979, disco music was becoming popular, but many people really hated it. So Veeck told

## SUPERSTAR!
# CARLOS QUENTIN

Quentin was on his way to a home-run title and a shot at the MVP until September 2008, when he punched his bat and broke his wrist! The young slugger struggled in 2009, but the Sox expect him to bounce back.

people to bring their disco records to the ballpark. Between the games of a doubleheader, he had the records piled on the field and burned. However, the fire got too big, the fans got too crazy, and the Sox had to forfeit the second game!

**You Can Look It Up!** CHICAGO'S OFFICIAL WEBSITE: www.whitesox.com

# CLEVELAND INDIANS

The Indians have a long history filled with terrific players and fond fan memories. They just don't have a lot of championships. They do have a great ballpark and—who knows?—maybe their time will come soon!

## GAME 1?
## 1901

The Cleveland ballclub was one of the original members of the AL. They were mostly called the Naps (after manager Napoleon Lajoie), before becoming the Indians in 1915.

## MAGIC MOMENT
### A New Ballpark

The Indians were considered a joke for decades, but a great new ballpark, opened in 1994, helped turn the team around.

## LOWEST LOW
### 1954 World Series

Cleveland won a then-AL-record 111 games, but were swept in the World Series by the New York Giants.

## STUFF

HOME:
**Progressive Field**

WORLD SERIES TITLES: **2**

ONLY IN CLEVELAND:
**Indians fan John Adams—pounding on his giant bass drum—has missed only a handful of games since 1973!**

## STAR SEASONS!

**1995** Albert Belle led the AL with 50 homers and 126 RBIs, helping Cleveland win the AL title.

**1999** Manny Ramirez knocked in 165 runs, the highest total by an American League player in 62 years!

**2008** Cliff Lee became the second consecutive Indians pitcher (after C.C. Sabathia) to win the Cy Young Award.

## The Ultimate Indian
# BOB FELLER

When "Rapid Robert" was just 17, he struck out 15 in his first game in the majors. Although he missed three seasons to serve in World War II, he was one of the best of all-time. He led the AL in wins six times and in strikeouts seven times—including a career-high of 348 in 1946—thanks to a 100-mph fastball.

**#1**

# FUNKY FACTS

➔ A sad fact: In 1920, Ray Chapman of the Indians was hit in the head by a pitch. He remains the only player in major league history to die as a result of an on-field injury.

➔ Cleveland's Municipal Stadium was so old and drafty that it was known as the "Mistake by the Lake." Lake Erie, that is.

➔ Were the Indians named after Louis "Chief" Sockalexis, a member of the Penobscot nation and a key player for the Cleveland Spiders in the 1890s? Legend says yes, but research shows that the name was cho-

## SUPERSTAR!
# GRADY SIZEMORE

*Baseball scouts look for players with the "five tools": speed, power, hitting for a high average, a strong throwing arm, and good glovework. This young All-Star is the prototypical five-tool player.*

sen in 1915 for other reasons.

➔ Slugger Rocky Colavito got into an argument with a rival fan before a 1959 game. Bad move by the fan: Colavito hit four homers in the game!

**You Can Look It Up!** CLEVELAND'S OFFICIAL WEBSITE: www.clevelandindians.com

# DETROIT
# TIGERS

The Tigers seem to tease their fans with great teams every few years, but they rarely win it all. Their last title came in 1984, though they've had several playoff teams since then. Will the Tigers roar in the future?

## GAME 1?
## 1901

The Tigers were one of the original members of the AL. They are among the few to keep their original name. The great Ty Cobb (1905–1926) was the Tigers' first superstar.

## 👍 MAGIC MOMENT
### 1984 Season

After starting the season with a stunning 35–5 record, the Tigers roared all year, winning their fourth World Series.

## 👎 LOWEST LOW
### 2003 Season

The Tigers lost an AL-record 119 games, including a nasty stretch at the start, when they lost 17 of their first 18 games.

## STUFF

HOME:
**Comerica Park**

WORLD SERIES TITLES: **4**

ONLY IN DETROIT:
**Comerica Park has a merry-go-round with tigers instead of horses, and a Ferris wheel with baseball-shaped cars!**

## STAR SEASONS!

**1968** Denny McLain became the last pitcher to win 30 games (he was 31–6) as the Tigers won the World Series.

**1984** Closer Willie Hernandez became only the seventh player to win both the MVP and Cy Young awards.

**2006** The Tigers won the AL title for the first time since their magical 1984 season.

## The Ultimate Tiger

# TY COBB

Cobb's 4,191 hits are the second-most ever. Until he was topped by Rickey Henderson, he was the all-time leader in runs scored, too. And his .366 career average remains the best ever. There was no one like Ty Cobb, before or since. His fierce style of play didn't win him friends, but his Tigers teammates loved him.

#1

# FUNKY FACTS

→ Detroit's Hank Greenberg was nearly the equal of Babe Ruth, at least for one season. The big first baseman smacked 58 homers in 1938. Greenberg was the first star major leaguer to join the army in the early days of World War II. He lost several seasons due to the war.

→ Second baseman Lou Whitaker and shortstop Alan Trammell played together for the first time in 1977. They were the Tigers' double-play combo for the next 18 years and a record 1,918 games.

→ In 1984, Detroit's Sparky Anderson became the first manager to lead a team from each league to a World Series championship. In 1975–1976,

## SUPERSTAR!
# MIGUEL CABRERA

*Some players were born to hit—Miguel Cabrera is one of them. No matter what pitchers try, he finds a way to beat them. He has five seasons with 30 HR/100 RBIs and led the AL with 37 homers in 2008.*

Anderson guided the Cincinnati Reds to back-to-back titles.

→ Fireballing pitcher Joel Zumaya missed three games in the 2005 playoffs after hurting his arm by playing too much Guitar Hero.

**You Can Look It Up!** DETROIT'S OFFICIAL WEBSITE: www.detroittigers.com

# KANSAS CITY ROYALS

The Royals had their moment in the sun, but they haven't made the playoffs since they won their only World Series in 1985. They do boast loyal fans and some good young players, so the sun may shine again.

## GAME 1?
## 1969

In 1969, the expansion Royals joined the AL West. They replaced the KC Athletics, who had just moved to Oakland. In 1994, the Royals moved to the new AL Central division.

 ## MAGIC MOMENT
### 1985 World Series

Playing their cross-state rivals, the St. Louis Cardinals, the Royals won the only World Series title in their history.

 ## LOWEST LOW
### Bottoming Out

The Royals lost at least 100 games in four of five seasons from 2002–2006, bottoming out with 106 losses in 2005.

## STUFF

HOME:
**Kauffman Stadium**

WORLD SERIES TITLES: **1**

ONLY IN KANSAS CITY:
**There is a 322-foot-wide waterfall behind the fence in left-center field. Home run balls don't land—they splash!**

## STAR SEASONS!

**1979** Speedy outfielder Willie Wilson led the AL with 83 stolen bases.

**1980** George Brett hit .390, the closest any player has come to .400 since 1941. Brett also was named the AL MVP.

**1994** In a season shortened by a labor dispute, David Cone won 16 games and a Cy Young Award.

## The Ultimate Royal
# GEORGE BRETT

A Gold Glove third base-man, one of the best pure hitters of the past 50 years, and one of baseball's nicest guys, Brett played a huge role in the Royals' only championship. He also won three batting titles—one each in the 1970s, 1980s, and 1990s. The Hall of Famer was a 13-time All-Star.

# FUNKY FACTS

➔ The Royals were one of the four expansion teams to join the majors in 1969. The others were the Pilots (who are now the Brewers), the Expos (now the Nationals), and the Padres. With 68 wins, KC had the best record of the four.

➔ The Royals boasted perhaps the shortest everyday player in baseball history. Freddie Patek was barely 5'5", but he was the team's regular shortstop for nine seasons in the 1970s.

➔ Bo Jackson was one of the best two-sport athletes ever. As an outfielder with the Royals (1986–1990), Jackson hit some of the longest home runs anyone could remember. He also had a great arm, once throwing from the warning track to home on the fly. In football, he was an electri-fying running back for the NFL's Oakland Raiders. He showed off his versatility in famous sneaker commercials, too.

## SUPERSTAR!
# ZACK GREINKE

The Royals thought this talented young pitcher would be a star a couple of years ago. He overcame some personal prob-lems to emerge in 2009 as the AL Cy Young Award winner. Better later than never!

**You Can Look It Up!** KANSAS CITY'S OFFICIAL WEBSITE: www.kansascityroyals.com

# MINNESOTA TWINS

With a new ballpark and some of the best young hitters in baseball, the Twins expect to add to a legacy that stretches back a century (not always in Minnesota). The team is the darling of the northern Midwest.

## GAME 1?
## 1901

The Washington Senators were an original member of the AL. In 1960, the team moved to Minnesota. It's named after its home, the Twin Cities of Minneapolis and St. Paul.

 ## MAGIC MOMENT
### 1987 World Series

The Twins had lost 91 games in 1986, so everyone—except the Twins—was stunned when the team won the World Series.

 ## LOWEST LOW
### Sad Senators

The Senators were terrible for a long time. Their worst season came in 1904, when they won only 38 games and lost 113!

## STUFF

HOME:
**Target Field**

WORLD SERIES TITLES: **3**

ONLY IN MINNESOTA:
**In the Twins' old ballpark, the marshmallow-like Metrodome, fans waved small, white "Homer Hankies."**

## STAR SEASONS!

**1924** Led by "The Big Train," right-hander Walter Johnson, the Senators won their only World Series title during their time in the nation's capital.

**1965** Shortstop Zoilo Versalles was an unlikely MVP as the Twins won the AL pennant.

**1969** The marvelous Rod Carew won the first of what would be seven AL batting titles.

## The Ultimate Twin
# KIRBY PUCKETT

With a fireplug of a body and the heart of a kid, Kirby Puckett led the Twins to two World Series titles, winning Game 6 in 1991 with an 11th-inning homer. Puckett had more hits in the 1990s than any other player. Sadly, his career was cut short by an eye disease, and he died in 2006 from heart disease.

# FUNKY FACTS

➜ A poem said that George Washington was "first in war, first in peace, and first in the hearts of his countrymen." The Senators were said to be "first in war, first in peace . . . and last in the American League."

➜ The biggest slugger in Twins history was first baseman Harmon "Killer" Killebrew. Despite his scary nickname, he was one of baseball's nicest guys—except to opposing pitchers. He crushed 573 homers in his Hall of Fame career.

➜ The Washington Senators enjoyed a fun baseball first on April 10, 1910. On Opening Day, William Howard Taft became the first president to throw out the ceremonial first

## SUPERSTAR!
# JOE MAUER

Catchers aren't supposed to hit, they're supposed to catch. No one told 2009 AL MVP Joe Mauer. He is the only catcher to win an AL batting title, which he's done three times (in 2006, 2008, and 2009).

pitch, a tradition which continues today for important games.

➜ The giant, plastic, right-field wall in the old Metrodome was known as "The Baggie."

**You Can Look It Up!** MINNESOTA'S OFFICIAL WEBSITE: www.minnesotatwins.com

# PITCHING!

**You, a baseball,** and 60 feet, six inches of distance to home plate. Your job? Pitch that baseball past the giant guy holding the big wooden stick. No problem, right? For more than a century, pitchers have been using every trick in the book (and a few that are not in the book, if you know what we mean) to fool hitters and get outs. In this chapter, we'll take a quick look at this difficult art and meet some of the superstars who have excelled as "moundsmen."

## INSIDE:

*Royals ace Zack Greinke shows awesome pitching form.*

# HOW TO PITCH

It looks so easy—just throw the ball as hard as you can and hit the catcher's mitt, right? Well, ask anyone who has tried to throw a baseball through a box that is 17 inches wide (the width of home plate) and as tall as the middle third of a batter. It's not as easy as it looks! This photo shows a few of the key things pitchers keep in mind as they try to mow down hitters.

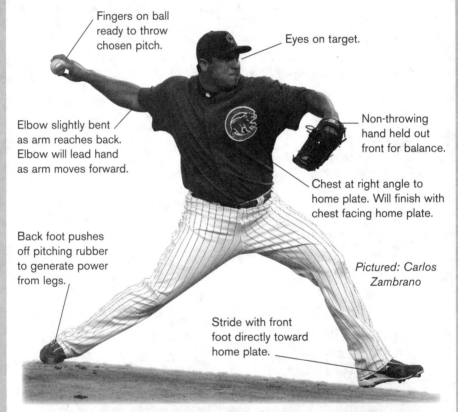

Fingers on ball ready to throw chosen pitch.

Eyes on target.

Elbow slightly bent as arm reaches back. Elbow will lead hand as arm moves forward.

Non-throwing hand held out front for balance.

Chest at right angle to home plate. Will finish with chest facing home plate.

Back foot pushes off pitching rubber to generate power from legs.

*Pictured: Carlos Zambrano*

Stride with front foot directly toward home plate.

## Why 60 Feet, Six Inches?

Today's pitchers stand exactly 60 feet, six inches from home plate. Before 1893, they stood only 50 feet away. Why the change? Pitcher Amos Rusie was so good, they moved all pitchers back to make it harder for them to strike people out!

# TYPES OF PITCHERS

In the early days of baseball, a team might have only one or two pitchers on its roster. Those poor guys would have to throw every inning, win or lose, easy day or ugly rout. Modern pitchers, however, are usually asked to fill just one specific role. Here's how today's big-league teams typically organize their pitchers.

## STARTERS
The big guns, they start every fifth game, taking turns in the pitching "rotation." They try to pitch at least six or seven innings, or more if they're doing well.

## LONG RELIEVERS
If a starter comes out early in the game, one of these guys steps in. He can pitch several innings in relief while his team tries to come back.

## SPECIALISTS
Some teams have a pitcher, usually a lefty, on hand to pitch to only one or two key batters, usually also lefties.

## SET-UP MEN
If a team is ahead in the seventh or eighth inning, a set-up man tries to hold that lead until it's the closer's turn to pitch.

## CLOSERS
The stars of the relief corps, they usually pitch only the ninth inning and only when the game is close. If they hold the lead and their team wins, they earn a "save."

# CURVES AND SLIDERS
# TYPES OF PITCHES

The pitcher's job is to fool the hitter. A smart pitcher doesn't just try to blow the batter away by throwing every pitch as hard as he can. Instead, he throws a variety of different pitches. The key to pitching is not so much speed—though that helps a lot!—as it is movement. Many of these pitches move in ways that make them very hard to hit. Here's a quick primer on the most popular pitches. The photos show how a pitcher grips them.

## Fastballs
Pitchers today use three basic types of fastballs, all of which are thrown with as much force as possible.

**✳4-seam:** This is the power pitch. It flies straight as an arrow, but its speed makes it a batter-beater!

**✳2-seam:** The fingers line up with the seams. It's not as fast as a 4-seam fastball, but it can sink or run in toward a right-handed batter.

**✳Split-finger:** This is slower than a 4- or 2-seamer, but it's thrown with the same arm motion as a regular fastball. The ball can drop quite a lot as it reaches the plate.

**✳Sinker:** This is a combination fastball/breaking ball. Thrown straighter than a curveball, it dips down very late.

## Breaking Balls
These pitches are designed to change direction on their way toward the plate. The grip and the motion of hand and wrist determine how they move.

**✳Curveball:** The classic breaking ball, it was supposedly "invented" by Candy Cummings in 1867. That's debated by experts, but a curveball's ability to fool gets no arguments. The pitcher twists his wrist toward the batter as he releases the ball. When thrown by a righty, the spin makes the ball curve, or "break," down and away from a right-handed batter.

# AND KNUCKLERS, OH MY!

★**Knuckleball:** Only a few hurlers throw this tricky pitch. The ball is held on the fingernails, not the knuckles. It is released straight ahead—and that's when things get weird. Knuckleballs do not go straight. They bob and dip and dart, with almost no spin. Both batters and catchers can look goofy trying to deal with these pitches.

★**Slider:** A faster pitch than a curveball, it has side-to-side movement. It's thrown with a wrist movement like opening a doorknob.

★**Screwball:** Rarely thrown today, this pitch is curved by twisting the wrist inward as the ball is released. It breaks in the opposite direction of a curveball.

## Change of Pace

This pitch fools the hitter not with movement, but with changes of speed.

★**Changeup:** A changeup is thrown with the same arm motion as a fastball but with a different grip that slows the ball down. This confuses the batter into thinking he's being thrown a fastball, which messes up his timing.

## THE STORY OF THE SPITBALL

Until 1920, it was legal in baseball to put, well . . . gunk on the ball. Pitchers used spit, tar, oil, mud, and shoe polish. They scratched, scraped, and tore the ball. Why? To make it move in weird and unpredictable ways. However, spitballs were also dangerous. A spitball was probably to blame for the only on-field death in baseball history. Ray Chapman was hit in the head by such a pitch in 1920 and died the next day. Following the 1920 season, baseball banned the practice of "doctoring" the ball. Pitchers caught throwing spitballs are now ejected from the game.

# FIGURING
# PITCHING

Numbers fly around ballparks like baseballs during batting practice. Just about every part of the game can be counted, added, divided, or multiplied in some way. Pitching is no exception. Every pitch a player throws is recorded. Here's a close-up look at two of the key stats that scouts, fans, and coaches use to compare pitchers.

## EARNED RUN AVERAGE (ERA)
## $(ER \times 9) \div IP = ERA$

This measures how many earned runs a pitcher would give up over a typical stretch of nine innings, or the length of a whole game. Pitchers with ERAs of less than 3.50 are very solid pitchers; elite hurlers can dip to near 2.50 or 2.00. To figure ERA, first you have to know how many of the runs that a pitcher allowed were earned. That means runs scored without help from errors. By counting only earned runs (and not, of course, "unearned" runs), pitchers are not penalized for mistakes made by their fielders.

Example: $(2 \text{ ER} \times 9) \div 7.33^* \text{ IP} = 2.46 \text{ ERA}$

*Partial innings are counted in thirds. So this pitcher threw seven full innings and one out of another inning.

## WALKS PLUS HITS PER INNING (WHIP)
## $(BB + H) \div IP = WHIP$

This statistic is popular in fantasy baseball. It measures how many opposing baserunners a pitcher allows—walks (BB) and hits (H)—in an average inning. Baserunners, of course, can become runs scored, so the fewer allowed the better. A really good WHIP is about 1.00. A pitcher with a WHIP above 2.00 is probably in danger of losing his job!

Example: $(3 \text{ BB} + 6 \text{ H}) \div 7.33 \text{ IP} = 1.23 \text{ WHIP}$

# TOP FIVES

Here's a look at the all-time bests in key career pitching statistics. Well, sort of all-time. Many baseball experts divide such stats into those made before or after 1901, when the American League became a major league. Also, we're ranking only starting pitchers who have reached a minimum total of 1,000 innings pitched in their careers.

## ERA

| | |
|---|---|
| Ed **WALSH** | 1.82 |
| Addie **JOSS** | 1.89 |
| Jack **PFIESTER** | 2.02 |
| "Smoky" Joe **WOOD** | 2.03 |
| "Three Finger" **BROWN** | 2.06 |

## WHIP

| | |
|---|---|
| Addie **JOSS** | 0.97 |
| Ed **WALSH** | 1.00 |
| Pedro **MARTINEZ***  | 1.05 |
| Christy **MATHEWSON** | 1.06 |
| Walter **JOHNSON** | 1.06 |

## WINS

| | |
|---|---|
| Cy **YOUNG** | 511 ▶▶▶ |
| Walter **JOHNSON** | 417 |
| Grover **ALEXANDER** | 373 |
| Christy **MATHEWSON** | 373 |
| Warren **SPAHN** | 363 |

*active player in 2009

# LOVE THOSE
# LEFTIES!

About ten percent of human beings are left-handed. But about 25 to 30 percent of major league pitchers are lefties. Here's a look at the best "southpaws" of all time.

### Lefty Grove, 1925–1941
Grove dominated the AL in the 1920s and 1930s. He won nine ERA and seven strikeout titles with the Athletics and Red Sox. His 31 wins in 1931 has been matched only once since.

### Warren Spahn, 1942, 1946–1965
Spahn pitched mostly for the Milwaukee/Atlanta Braves, and he ended his long career with more wins than any other lefty: 363. Spahn also led the NL in wins eight times.

### Sandy Koufax, 1955–1966
The last seven seasons of this Dodger star's career were simply incredible. He won three Cy Young awards, five straight ERA titles, posted 25 or more wins three times, and set a single-season record (since broken) with 382 strikeouts in 1965.

### Steve "Lefty" Carlton, 1965–1988
A four-time Cy Young winner, Carlton was a great pitcher on some bad teams. In 1972, he won 27 games . . . all the other Phillies pitchers combined won only 32!

### ◄◄◄Randy Johnson, 1988–
The best lefty in the game for the past two decades, the "Big Unit" is also one of the tallest ever at 6'10". He has won five Cy Young awards, including four in a row from 1999–2002. He has nine strikeout titles.

## WHY "SOUTHPAW"?

Left-handed pitchers are sometimes called by that nickname. It comes from when all baseball games were played in daylight. To keep the afternoon sun out of the batters' eyes, most diamonds were built facing east. That meant a left-handed pitcher's throwing arm was pointed . . . south!

# FAMOUS KNUCKLERS

The knuckleball (see page 61) is one of the weirdest things in baseball. Only a few players in history have mastered this dancing, darting devil to win a lot of games. Here's a quick look at history's best knucklers.

**Eddie Cicotte, 1905, 1908–1920** Until he was caught in the 1919 Black Sox scandal (see page 141), Cicotte was the best knuckleballer in the game. He led the AL in wins twice and had a career 2.38 ERA.

**Phil Niekro, 1964–1987** Knuckleball pitchers often have long careers because the pitch is not as hard on their arms. Niekro played 24 seasons in his Hall of Fame career, mostly with the Braves. He won 318 games with three 20-win seasons. He also had a pair of 20-loss seasons—which just shows how hard the knuckleball can be to control.

**Charlie Hough, 1970–1994** Hough (pronounced "HUFF") was another knuckler who stuck around. He was still floating them in there when he was 46 years old.

**Hoyt Wilhelm, 1952–1972** When he retired, Wilhelm had appeared in more games (1,070) than any other pitcher in history. (His record has since been topped.) He was both a reliever and starter.

**Tim Wakefield, 1992–93, 1995– ▶▶▶**
After realizing he'd never make his dreams of being a first baseman come true, Wakefield has used a nasty knuckler to forge a long career. He has been a dependable part of the Red Sox rotation since 1995, helping them win two World Series titles. In 2009, at the age of 42, he became a first-time All-Star!

# THE FASTEST EVER

The debate over who is the fastest pitcher of all time (or should we say, who threw the fastest pitches?) will rage as long as we play baseball. There's no real answer, but here are some very popular candidates.

### WALTER **JOHNSON**
Nicknamed "The Big Train" for his high-speed fastball.

### ◀◀◀BOB **FELLER**
"Rapid Robert" claimed to have reached 107 mph.

### NOLAN **RYAN**
You pitch seven no-hitters, you get on this list.

### RANDY **JOHNSON**
At 6'10", he's almost unfair to hitters.

### BILLY **WAGNER**
He makes the list for being a little guy with a 100-mph heater.

## RADAR LOVE

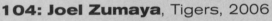

With radar guns trained on every pitch, some stunning numbers do pop up. Not all radar guns are the same, so you have to take these figures with a grain of salt. However, here are the fastest speeds recorded during major league games:

**104: Joel Zumaya**, Tigers, 2006

**103: Mark Wohlers**, Braves, 1993

**102*: Jonathan Broxton**, Dodgers, 2009

*Matched by six others; Broxton's pitch is the most recent.

# PERFECT GAMES

A quarterback who completes all his passes can still lose. A basketball player who doesn't miss a shot can be on the losing team. But a pitcher who is "perfect" is a guaranteed winner. A perfect game is one in which the starting pitcher does not allow a single baserunner: no hits, no walks, no errors . . . and of course, no runs. Here are the 18 pitchers who have accomplished this rare feat.

*Buehrle: the most recent "perfecto"*

| PITCHER, TEAM | YEAR |
|---|---|
| **J. Lee Richmond,** Ruby Legs | 1880 |
| **John Ward,** Providence Grays | 1880 |
| **Cy Young,** Red Sox | 1904 |
| **Addie Joss,** Cleveland Naps | 1908 |
| **Charlie Robertson,** White Sox | 1922 |
| **Don Larsen,** Yankees | 1956 |
| **Jim Bunning,** Phillies | 1964 |
| **Sandy Koufax,** Dodgers | 1965 |
| **Jim "Catfish" Hunter,** Athletics | 1968 |
| **Len Barker,** Indians | 1981 |
| **Mike Witt,** Angels | 1984 |
| **Tom Browning,** Reds | 1988 |
| **Dennis Martinez,** Expos | 1991 |
| **Kenny Rogers,** Rangers | 1994 |
| **David Wells,** Yankees | 1998 |
| **David Cone,** Yankees | 1999 |
| **Randy Johnson,** Diamondbacks | 2004 |
| **Mark Buehrle,** White Sox | 2009 |

# HERO TIME

## Christy Mathewson

**In 2006,** a group of baseball experts put together lists of the top 20 pitchers of all time. I was one of those experts, and I put the player known as "Matty" on the top of my list.

In a time when baseball players were regarded as hard-living scoundrels, when few were well-schooled or well-spoken, Mathewson stood out as a

popular, college-educated athlete. He was also stunningly good. He is tied for third all-time with 373 wins and is among the best ever in ERA (2.13) and shutouts (79). During the 1905 World Series against the Philadelphia Athletics, Matty put together one of the greatest baseball feats of all time. He pitched three shutouts in six days, allowing only one walk while striking out 18.

With the New York Giants from 1900–1916, he became the United States' most popular athlete, the subject of books and even films. Sadly, the great hero died young, at age 45 in 1925, a delayed victim of a poison gas accident while training for World War I.

# Nolan Ryan

**The story** of the fireballing Ryan Express runs on two tracks. The first is a fast one—that's how Nolan Ryan pitched. Fast. The big Texan blew into baseball in 1966 with one of the most powerful fastballs anyone had ever seen. The problem was, he wasn't always sure where it was going. The second track is a slow one—that's because Nolan Ryan finally figured out the strike zone and stuck around to pitch for a major league record 27 years.

He ended up with 5,714 strikeouts, still the most ever by nearly 1,000. He had six seasons with more than 300 "punchouts," including the all-time single-season record of 383 in 1973. He also threw a stunning total of seven no-hitters. No one else even has five. Ryan pitched for the Mets, Angels, Astros, and Rangers in his long career. Today, he's the president of the Rangers and loves helping young pitchers try to climb on the Express . . . but he'll remain that train's only first-class passenger.

# LOS ANGELES
# ANGELS OF ANAHEIM

Okay, they have a long name that includes two cities. But they have one thing that some expansion teams don't: a World Series title. A big sports magazine also called the Angels the best organization in sports. Not bad!

## GAME 1?
## 1961

First they were the LA Angels. Then they became the California Angels and moved to Anaheim. Then they were the Anaheim Angels. Then their current name. Whew.

 ## MAGIC MOMENT
### 2002 World Series

An amazing comeback in Game 6 over the Barry Bonds-led Giants led to a Game 7 victory at home and the title.

## LOWEST LOW
### 1986 ALCS

The Angels were one strike away from the World Series when the Red Sox came from behind to win the game and the series.

## STUFF

**HOME:**
Angel Stadium

**WORLD SERIES TITLES: 1**

**ONLY IN ANAHEIM:**
One of the stadium's nicknames is "The Big A." So there's a giant metal letter *A* in the parking lot.

## STAR SEASONS!

**1973** Nolan Ryan set an all-time record by striking out 383 hitters, one of seven times he led the AL as an Angel.

**1979** Don Baylor became the first designated hitter to win the AL MVP award.

**2000** With 47 homers, third baseman Troy Glaus was the first Angels player to lead the league for a full season.

## The Ultimate Angel

# TIM SALMON

The 1993 AL Rookie of the Year, Salmon played his entire career with the Angels, retiring in style four years after the team won the 2002 World Series. He's the team's all-time leader in many batting categories, including homers with 299. A rocket-armed outfielder, Salmon oddly was never an All-Star.

**#1**

# FUNKY FACTS

→ Great start: In 1962, Angels rookie Bo Belinsky threw a no-hitter. He became more famous, though, for all the celebrities he hung out with while he played in LA.

→ Is there an "Angels Curse"? Sadly, several members of the team have died in off-field accidents over the years. There was even a bus crash that knocked the manager out for the season.

→ In 2000, the Angels were trailing the Giants when a video of a dancing monkey appeared on the JumboTron. The Angels rallied, and the "Rally Monkey" was born. Fans still wave stuffed monkeys whenever the Angels need a comeback.

### SUPERSTAR!

# TORII HUNTER

In 2009, Hunter earned his ninth career Gold Glove Award, thanks to another season of wall-climbing, homer-robbing center-field action. The veteran also has eight 20-HR seasons.

→ The Angels are owned by Arte Moreno, a billboard billionaire who became the first Latino owner of a major league team in 2003.

**You Can Look It Up!** LA'S OFFICIAL WEBSITE: www.angels.mlb.com

# OAKLAND
# ATHLETICS

Three cities, incredible superstars, and Connie Mack, to say nothing of white elephants, orange baseballs, and a donkey for a mascot. You can't say that life with the Athletics is ever boring.

## GAME 1?
## 1901

The Philadelphia A's began life as one of the AL's original franchises. A stint in Kansas City from 1955–1967 was uneventful. They moved to Oakland in 1968, and things got fun!

 ## MAGIC MOMENT
### 1974 World Series

The A's beat the Dodgers to become the only team other than the Yankees to win three straight World Series.

 ## LOWEST LOW
### A Bad Year

In 1916, two years after they made the World Series, the A's sold off their best players and lost 117 games!

## STUFF

**HOME:**
**Oakland-Alameda County Coliseum**

**WORLD SERIES TITLES: 9**

**ONLY IN OAKLAND:**
**Pitchers love Oakland! The largest foul territory of any ballpark makes room for lots of pop outs.**

## STAR SEASONS!

### 1910
Pitcher Jack Coombs won three games to help the Athletics win the first World Series title in their history.

### 1933
Jimmie Foxx won the Triple Crown. He led the AL in homers, RBIs, and average.

### 1989
In an all-Bay Area World Series interrupted by an earthquake, Oakland beat San Francisco in four games.

## The Ultimate Athletic

# CONNIE MACK

With a nod toward A's sluggers Jimmie Foxx and Sal Bando, there's only one name that belongs here: Cornelius McGillicuddy. Known as Connie Mack, he was the team's owner and manager for its first 50 years! He led the "Mackmen" to five World Series titles. Mack's 3,731 wins as a manager are far and away the most ever.

# FUNKY FACTS

→ Longtime A's owner Connie Mack hired himself to be the manager every year. He was famous for wearing a business suit in the dugout instead of a uniform.

→ Charlie Finley owned the A's from 1960–1980 and was full of weird ideas. He paid his players to grow mustaches, suggested they use orange baseballs, and hired a donkey as a mascot.

→ Why do the A's wear arm patches decorated with white elephants? Way back in 1901, famed New York Giants manager John McGraw called the A's "white elephants." He meant that they were more trouble than they were worth. The A's showed him, beating McGraw's Giants in the World Series in 1911 and 1913.

## SUPERSTAR!
# RAJAI DAVIS

This speedy young outfielder is bringing the art of the steal back to Oakland, longtime home of base-stealing king Rickey Henderson. Davis had at least 25 steals every season from 2007–2009.

**You Can Look It Up!** OAKLAND'S OFFICIAL WEBSITE: www.oaklandathletics.com

# SEATTLE
# MARINERS

The Mariners have had some superstar players (Ken Griffey Jr., Randy Johnson, Edgar Martinez, Ichiro Suzuki), but they haven't put together enough of them to reach the World Series. The Northwest still waits!

## GAME 1?
## 1977

The Mariners were an expansion team in 1977, along with the Toronto Blue Jays. Seattle's team took its name from the city's long connection to the water.

 ## MAGIC MOMENT
### Safe at Home

Ken Griffey Jr. slid home with the winning run as the Mariners upset the Yankees in the 1995 AL division series.

 ## LOWEST LOW
### How'd It Happen?

A year after finishing second in the AL West, the Mariners lost 101 games in 2008, their worst season since 1983.

## STUFF

HOME:
**Safeco Field**

WORLD SERIES TITLES: 0

ONLY IN SEATTLE:
**Safeco's roof can close in ten minutes, allowing games to continue despite Seattle's frequent rainstorms.**

## STAR SEASONS!

**1995** Randy Johnson was the Cy Young Award winner, going 18–2 with 294 strikeouts.

**1996** In just his third year in the majors, superstar Alex Rodriguez led the AL with a .358 batting average.

**2004** The incredible Ichiro Suzuki set a new single-season record by rapping out 262 hits.

## The Ultimate Mariner
# EDGAR MARTINEZ

He rarely used his glove (he played third base when he did), but this *Ultimate* Mariner has a shot at the Hall of Fame . . . as perhaps the best designated hitter ever. Martinez had a .312 career average and twice led the AL in batting. He's Seattle's all-time leader in games, runs, hits, and RBIs.

**#1**

# FUNKY FACTS

→ The Mariners were not the first major league team in Seattle. The Pilots played there for one season (1969), before moving to Milwaukee to become the Brewers.

→ Seattle's mascot is the Mariners Moose, who joined the team in 1990. In 2007, he almost got in big trouble. While speeding around the field (between innings) on his go-cart, he bonked into Red Sox outfielder Coco Crisp. Crisp wasn't hurt, but the Moose had to slow down for a while!

→ In 1990, Seattle's Ken Griffey Sr. and Jr. became the only father-son duo to play in the same outfield. They once hit homers in back-to-back at-bats.

## SUPERSTAR!
# ICHIRO SUZUKI

Perhaps the best pure hitter in baseball, Ichiro led Japan's Pacific League in batting seven times. Since joining Seattle in 2001, he's had at least 200 hits in every season and won two AL batting titles.

→ Do you like sushi? (You know what sushi is, right? It's a Japanese food made from fish.) At Mariners games, fans can enjoy a star-inspired "Ichiroll."

**You Can Look It Up!** SEATTLE'S OFFICIAL WEBSITE: www.seattlemariners.com

# TEXAS
# RANGERS

Often blessed with elite sluggers, the Rangers have struggled to find enough pitching to do well in the tough AL West. However, some young talent and a homer-friendly ballpark mean big things are ahead in Texas!

## GAME 1?
## 1961

The Rangers are, along with the Twins, formerly known as the Washington Senators. The team that became the Rangers started in D.C. in 1961 and moved to Texas in 1972.

 ## MAGIC MOMENT
### Perfect Kenny

Kenny Rogers pitched a perfect game on July 28, 1994, one of only six ever thrown by a left-handed pitcher.

 ## LOWEST LOW
### Go Back to D.C.?

Texas fans must have thought their new team was a lemon. In 1973, the Rangers lost 105 games!

## STUFF

HOME:
**Rangers Ballpark in Arlington**

WORLD SERIES TITLES: 0

ONLY IN ARLINGTON:
**The Rangers have a kid-sized ballpark right next door that fans can rent for birthday parties!**

## STAR SEASONS!

**1968** The Senators weren't that good, but big Frank Howard did lead the AL with 44 home runs.

**1992** Catcher Ivan Rodriguez won the first of the ten Gold Gloves he would win with Texas (out of his 13 overall).

**2008** Outfielder Josh Hamilton was a surprise AL RBI leader with 130.

## The Ultimate Ranger
# JUAN GONZALEZ

They like to do things BIG in Texas, so Juan Gonzalez fit right in. During his 13 seasons with the Rangers, he had five seasons with 40 homers (and one with 39!). Known as "Juan Gone" for his power, Gonzalez was the AL MVP in 1996 and 1998. He set a team record with 157 RBIs in 1998.

**#1**

# FUNKY FACTS

➜ The great Ted Williams was lured out of his favorite fishing holes to manage the Senators in 1969. He moved with the team to Texas and led them during their first season there.

➜ In 1991, Nolan Ryan became the oldest pitcher ever to throw a no-hitter, when he blanked the Toronto Blue Jays at the age of 44!

➜ The Rangers were once partly owned by the 43rd president, George W. Bush. He helped run the team before he became governor of Texas.

➜ Rangers slugger Jose Canseco hit a lot of homers, including one without a bat. In

## SUPERSTAR!
# JOSH HAMILTON

Hamilton overcame drug problems to return to the ballpark. He led the AL in RBIs during his fantastic 2008 season. With all the baseball tools, he should be a star for a long time.

a 1993 game, he ran back to catch a ball hit by Cleveland's Carlos Martinez. But the ball hit Canseco's head and bounced over the wall. Home run!

**You Can Look It Up!** TEXAS'S OFFICIAL WEBSITE: www.texasrangers.com

# ATLANTA BRAVES

Thanks to a national cable TV channel, the Braves have fans around the country. The team is continuing a tradition that stretches back more than 130 years, with time spent in three cities.

## GAME 1?
## 1871

The Boston Red Stockings were founded in 1871, five years before the NL began. The team moved to Milwaukee in 1953, before ending up in Atlanta in 1966.

 ## MAGIC MOMENT
### 1995 World Series

The Braves captured the first of their 11 straight NL East titles and won their only World Series championship in Atlanta.

 ## LOWEST LOW
### Grounded Birds

The team was called the Doves (see Funky Facts) when it set a franchise record with 108 losses way back in 1909.

## STUFF

HOME:
**Turner Field**

WORLD SERIES TITLES: **3**

ONLY IN ATLANTA:
**Fans often serenade their team by chanting as they wave their hands and foam axes in the "Tomahawk Chop."**

## STAR SEASONS!

**1914** The "Miracle Braves" were in last place in July but roared back to win the World Series.

**1957** Pitcher Lew Burdette won three games as the Braves knocked off the Yankees in the Series.

**1999** Longtime Braves favorite Chipper Jones won the NL MVP award, batting .319 and hitting 45 homers.

## The Ultimate Brave
# HANK AARON

This was an easy choice. Until 2007, "Hammerin' Hank" was the all-time home-run leader with 755. He led the NL in hitting twice and in RBIs four times. He also had eight seasons with 40 or more homers. Aaron has been involved with the team off the field for years, and he's one of baseball's most beloved men.

**#1**

# FUNKY FACTS

➔ The team was dubbed the Braves in 1912. Some of their earlier names were the Red Caps, Beaneaters, Doves, and Rustlers. And they were briefly known as the Bees.

➔ Braves legend Hank Aaron holds lots of records for his hitting. For one of them, he needed help. He and Tommie Aaron hold the record for most career homers by brothers: 755 for Hank and 13 for Tommie!

➔ Media magnate Ted Turner owned the Braves in the 1970s. The team was so bad in 1977 that Turner fired the manager during a long losing streak and took over for one game. He lost and got a baseball man the next day!

## SUPERSTAR!
# DEREK LOWE

The veteran right-hander joined the Braves in 2009 and quickly became the staff ace. The former Dodgers and Red Sox hurler led the Braves with 15 wins.

➔ The first issue of *Sports Illustrated* came out on August 16, 1954. It featured Braves slugger Eddie Mathews swinging for the fences on the cover.

**You Can Look It Up!** ATLANTA'S OFFICIAL WEBSITE: www.atlantabraves.com

## FLORIDA
# MARLINS

The Marlins were the first team to play full-time in Florida, the longtime home of spring training for many baseball teams. For such a young franchise, the Marlins have had lots of success, winning two titles.

## GAME 1?
# 1993

The Marlins were named an expansion team by Major League Baseball. The first pitch in franchise history was a knuckleball, thrown by veteran Charlie Hough.

 **MAGIC MOMENT**
### 1997 World Series

An 11th-inning single by Edgar Renteria made the Marlins the world champions in only their fifth season.

 **LOWEST LOW**
### Crash!

The year after the Marlins won it all, they set an unhappy record: Most losses by a defending World Series champ—108!

## STUFF

HOME:
**Land Shark Stadium**

WORLD SERIES TITLES: **2**

ONLY IN MIAMI:
**Wondering about the Land Shark name? It comes from a tune written by singer (and team co-owner) Jimmy Buffett.**

# STAR SEASONS!

**1995** A pinch-hit homer by Florida's Jeff Conine made him the MVP of the All-Star Game.

**2003** Josh Beckett pitched a shutout in Game 6 to close out the Yankees and give the Marlins their second title.

**2009** Outstanding shortstop Hanley Ramirez became the first Marlin to lead the NL in batting.

## The Ultimate Marlin
# LUIS CASTILLO

A team this young doesn't have a lot of history, but Castillo was part of nearly all of it. The team's all-time leader in runs, games, and hits, Castillo helped the Marlins win two World Series while twice leading the NL in steals. He's a three-time All-Star and has won three Gold Gloves. He played for the Mets in 2009.

# FUNKY FACTS

→ The Marlins won only 64 games in their expansion season in 1993. Closer Bryan Harvey was on the mound for the final out in most of them. He saved 45 of the wins and made the All-Star team.

→ Dominican native Luis Castillo had a 35-game hitting streak in 2002. It was the longest hitting streak ever by a second baseman, and the longest streak ever by a player born outside the United States.

→ Marlins mascot Billy The Marlin once tried to parachute into a game. One problem: His costume head fell off before he landed. So he steered away from the ballpark. The head was later found by the side of a highway.

## SUPERSTAR!
# HANLEY RAMIREZ

When fantasy baseball owners choose their teams, this all-around star is drafted quickly. He hits for a high average, steals bases, and plays outstanding defense.

→ Since the team plays in stormy Florida, all the glass in the Marlins' new ballpark set to open in 2012 will be guaranteed hurricane-proof!

**You Can Look It Up!** FLORIDA'S OFFICIAL WEBSITE: www.floridamarlins.com

# NEW YORK METS

The Mets play in the shadow of the Yankees' 27 World Series titles. However, the Mets have some of their own championship hardware and a corps of devoted fans. And they have a beautiful new ballpark, too!

## GAME 1?
## 1962

The New York Giants and Brooklyn Dodgers moved west in 1958, leaving the Yankees alone in New York City. That ended when the Metropolitans started playing in 1962.

 ## MAGIC MOMENT
### 1969 World Series

The "Miracle Mets" surprised everyone but their fans as they beat the highly favored Orioles to win their first World Series.

 ## LOWEST LOW
### Slow Start

The Mets didn't exactly charge out of the gate. In their debut season, they set an NL record by losing 120 games!

## STUFF

HOME:
**Citi Field**

WORLD SERIES TITLES: **2**

ONLY IN QUEENS:
**The entry to Citi Field, which opened in 2009, honors a ballplayer from another team, the Dodgers' Jackie Robinson.**

## STAR SEASONS!

**1973** Led by fiery reliever Tug McGraw, who cried "Ya gotta believe!" the Mets won their second NL pennant.

**1986** Down to their last out, the Mets rallied to beat Boston in Game 6 of the World Series, and won it all in Game 7.

**2000** The Mets got a shot at their crosstown rivals, but the Yanks won the Subway Series.

# The Ultimate Met
# TOM SEAVER

When Tom Seaver was up for the Hall of Fame in 1992, he got the highest percentage of votes ever. Everybody loved this big, hard-throwing right-hander, but no one loved him more than Mets fans. "Tom Terrific" pitched in New York for 11 seasons and won three Cy Young awards, three ERA titles, and five strikeout crowns.

# FUNKY FACTS

➜ The wonderful Casey Stengel managed the first Mets team in 1962. A legend in New York after leading the Yankees to seven World Series titles, not even Stengel could whip the sorry Mets into shape.

➜ The Mets' old home at Shea Stadium was right next to LaGuardia Airport. When planes flew over, batters had to step out of the box to avoid being distracted by the noise.

➜ "Marvelous" Marv Throneberry was a terrible baserunner. He was once called out for missing first base after hitting a triple. Stengel went out to argue, but was told, "Don't bother, he missed second base, too."

## SUPERSTAR!
# DAVID WRIGHT

Though his production dipped in 2009, David Wright is the total package. A solid defensive third baseman, the four-time All-Star also has power and speed (three seasons with 20 or more steals).

➜ The Mets are one of the few teams with a fight song. They play "Meet the Mets, meet the Mets, step right up and greet the Mets" at games.

**You Can Look It Up!** NEW YORK'S OFFICIAL WEBSITE: www.newyorkmets.com

# PHILADELPHIA
# PHILLIES

The Phillies have been in the same city with the same nickname longer than any other team in baseball. They also did the same thing a lot—lose. However, in the past few seasons, Philly has emerged as an NL powerhouse.

## GAME 1?
## 1883

The Philadelphia Quakers were named after a group of colonists who helped found the state of Pennsylvania. The team changed its name to the Phillies in 1890.

 ## MAGIC MOMENT
### 1980 World Series

An entire city leaped with joy after reliever Tug McGraw got the final out to clinch the team's first World Series title.

 ## LOWEST LOW
### War Years

After the Phillies lost 100+ games annually from 1938–1942, they changed their name to the Blue Jays for two years. It didn't help.

## STUFF

**HOME:**
**Citizens Bank Park**

**WORLD SERIES TITLES: 2**

**ONLY IN PHILADELPHIA:**
**A giant neon Liberty Bell on the stadium scoreboard moves back and forth to "ring" after Phillies home runs.**

## STAR SEASONS!

**1915** The Phillies made their only World Series appearance from 1883–1949. They lost.

**1933** Chuck Klein won the NL Triple Crown, leading the league in homers, RBIs, and average.

**1972** Steve "Lefty" Carlton won 27 games and the first of his four Cy Young awards. The team's other pitchers went 32–87!

## The Ultimate Phillie
# MIKE SCHMIDT

When baseball fans argue about who was the best at each position, third base is the shortest argument. Michael Jack Schmidt is the hands-down winner. Not only did he win ten Gold Gloves for fielding excellence, he also smashed 548 homers, leading the NL in that category eight times.

**#1**

# FUNKY FACTS

➔ The great 1950 Phillies won the NL pennant. Filled with young stars, they were nicknamed the "Whiz Kids."

➔ Philly held a commanding six-and-a-half-game lead with 12 to play in 1964. But it managed to lose enough of them to blow the NL pennant. The disaster was called the Philly Phold.

➔ In 2008, Phillies closer Brad Lidge didn't blow a save. He didn't lose a game, either . . . except for the All-Star Game!

➔ The Phillies boast the majors' most famous and funniest mascot—the long-snouted,

## SUPERSTAR!
# RYAN HOWARD

*Big Ryan Howard is one of the most feared sluggers in the game. He won the 2006 MVP and helped the Phillies win the 2008 World Series. He's a two-time NL home-run champ.*

green-furred, monster-of-no-specific-species Phillie Phanatic. He rides a motor scooter, goofs around with players, and entertains fans in the stands.

**You Can Look It Up!** PHILADELPHIA'S OFFICIAL WEBSITE: www.philadelphiaphillies.com

# WASHINGTON
# NATIONALS

Our capital's team used to play in another country! That's right—until 2004, the Washington Nationals were the Montreal Expos, the pride of French Canada. But in 2005, the team said *au revoir* and moved to Washington, D.C.

## GAME 1?
## 1969

*Bonjour, les Expos!* Welcome to Canada! The team was named for Expo '67, a huge international fair held in Montreal as the team was being planned.

 ## MAGIC MOMENT
### Perfecto!

In 1991, Dennis Martinez beat the Dodgers with a perfect game. He was the first Latino pitcher to achieve this rare feat.

 ## LOWEST LOW
### Bad in Both Eras

As the Expos, they lost 110 games in 1969. In the franchise's 40th season in 2008, the Nationals managed to lose 102!

## STUFF

**HOME:**
**Nationals Park**

**WORLD SERIES TITLES: 0**

**ONLY IN D.C.:**
**Nationals Park, which opened in 2008, was the first MLB stadium to get an award for being environmentally friendly.**

## STAR SEASONS!

**1969** The Expos won the first major league game ever played in Canada, defeating the St. Louis Cardinals 8–7.

**1981** In a strike-interrupted season, the Expos came within a game of the World Series.

**1997** Pedro Martinez won the NL Cy Young Award, going 17–8 with a sparkling 1.90 ERA.

## The Ultimate Expo
# TIM RAINES

Sorry, Nationals. You've only been a team for a few seasons, so we're going to go back in your franchise history to name your *ultimate* player. Andre Dawson and Tim Wallach get votes, but we'll go with seven-time All-Star "Rock" Raines, a batting champ and four-time NL steals champ for the Expos.

**#1**

# FUNKY FACTS

➜ An early Expos favorite was left-handed hitter Rusty Staub. Due to his flaming red hair, he was known in French Canada as "*Le Grande Orange.*"

➜ The only time the Expos finished in first, they didn't get a chance to be in the playoffs. In 1994, the season ended in August due to a labor dispute. The Expos had the best record in the majors, but the playoffs and World Series were canceled.

➜ In 2009, pitcher Joel Hanrahan earned a win for the Nats . . . while he was with Pittsburgh! He had been traded by Washington soon after being taken out of a tie game that was halted by rain. When the game

## SUPERSTAR!
# RYAN ZIMMERMAN

*Third baseman Ryan Zimmerman is one of the young stars the Nationals hope to build around. The 2009 All-Star has hit 20 homers in three of his six seasons. And he's only 25!*

was completed two months later, he got credit for the win!

➜ The Expos had a very odd mascot, a weird, orange-and-blue thing named Youppi.

**You Can Look It Up!** WASHINGTON'S OFFICIAL WEBSITE: www.nationals.com

# DEFENSE & BASERUNNING

**We've seen hitting and pitching.** What happens next? Once the ball is hit, the game changes from a one-on-one battle to a nine-on-one defensive struggle. The fielders chase the ball to make outs and prevent batters from becoming baserunners. In this chapter, we'll look at fancy glovework on defense, meet some of baseball's best ever at "flashing the leather," and find out how speedy baserunners can turn a baseball game into a track meet!

## INSIDE:

*Crash! A.J. Pierzynski tries to bowl over this Cubs catcher.*

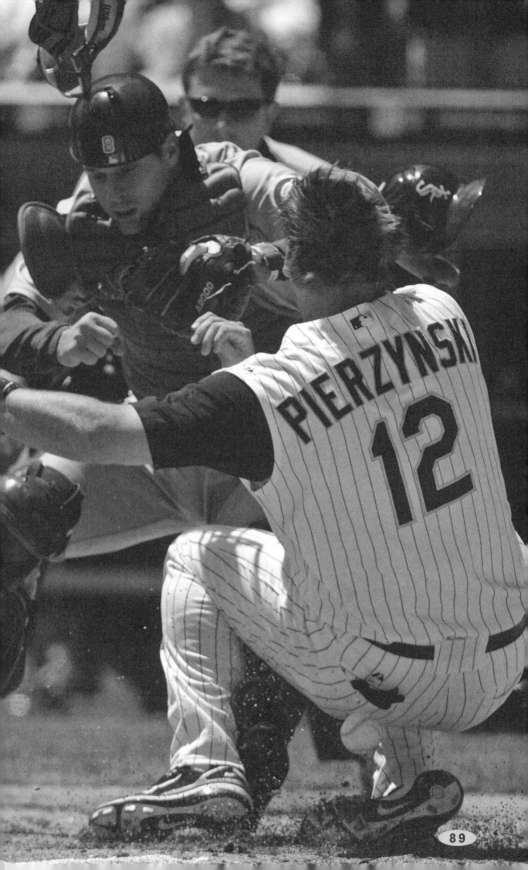

# AROUND THE
# DIAMOND

Each player in the field has an assigned area to cover. Job No. 1 is to retrieve balls that come into that area. Then the player throws it wherever it will do his team the most good. Each position calls for specific skills. Here's a look at some of the basics of each position. Note: The numbers in parentheses are used to track defensive plays while keeping score. (See page 92.)

## PITCHER (1)
As soon as the pitch leaves his hand, he's a fielder. A pitcher gets his glove up quickly to snag line drives. If a grounder is hit to the right side, the pitcher sprints to first base to cover for the first baseman. The pitcher also helps field bunts near the mound. And he backs up third base or home plate on throws from the outfield.

## CATCHER (2)
This heavily padded warrior has the hardest defensive job. He has to catch whatever the pitcher throws. He also helps "call" the game (choose what pitches will be thrown). And he chases down foul pops. The catcher throws to bases to cut down potential base stealers, and he springs out of his crouch to field bunts near home plate. When a baserunner tries to score, the catcher's job is to block the plate, catch the throw home, and tag out the runner. The catcher also passes along signals from the coaches to fielders.

## FIRST BASE (3)
Helped by a giant mitt, he catches or scoops up throws from other infielders on the most common baseball play, the infield groundout. He also fields grounders in his area, throwing to second to start double plays or tossing to the pitcher covering first. He also chases foul pops. A first baseman is usually a big guy who gives infielders a good target. On throws from the outfield, he acts as a cutoff man, catching the outfield throw and relaying it to another base.

## SECOND BASE (4)

Fielding grounders and line drives and chasing down short fly balls are just part of a second baseman's job. He's also responsible, with the shortstop, for covering second on double plays and attempted steals. He also covers second on balls hit to center and left field. He probably doesn't have as strong of a throwing arm as the shortstop or third baseman, but he has to be athletic enough to chase down balls hit between first and second base.

## THIRD BASE

(5) It's called the "hot corner" for a reason. This infielder sets up closer to the batter than anyone but the pitcher and catcher. The third baseman has to be ready for both screaming line drives and little rolling bunts. He has to throw across the diamond to first, so he needs a strong arm. He also covers his base on steal attempts and chases down pop ups near the stands.

## SHORTSTOP

(6) The shortstop is usually the finest defensive player on a team. The position was not part of baseball for its first 20 years or so, but it was a wise addition! A shortstop ranges across his area to grab ground balls and make quick, powerful throws to first. He also works with the second baseman on double plays and helps cover second base on steal attempts. A shortstop can range all the way to the left-field line to chase down fly balls. On hits to center and left field, he might help as a cutoff man.

## LEFT FIELD, CENTER FIELD, RIGHT FIELD

(7) (8) (9) Whether they catch the ball in the air or pick it up off the ground, outfielders track down every ball hit their way and quickly throw it back into the infield. The center fielder is the quarterback of the outfield. He calls off his fellow fielders when he can make the play, and he backs up his teammates when the ball is hit to them. He backs up second base when a runner tries to steal. The right fielder usually has the strongest arm, since he makes the longest outfield throw, from his corner to third base. The most spectacular outfield plays are diving catches and leaps at the wall to rob batters of homers.

# KEEPING SCORE

In baseball, a series of codes, letters, and numbers can be used to represent the results of each at-bat. Position numbers and codes are recorded on scoresheets to follow the action. It used to be that many people "scored" a game; today, it's a dying art. At right are the most common codes used for keeping score (see pages 90–91 for position numbers).

*The scoresheet for a set of four batters is below. Each box is one batter. The corners of each box are the diamond, with home plate at bottom left.*

| | |
|---|---|
| — | = single |
| = | = double |
| ≡ | = triple |
| K | = strikeout |
| BB | = base on balls (walk) |
| E | = error |
| FC | = fielder's choice |
| SB | = stolen base |
| CS | = caught stealing |
| WP | = wild pitch |
| PB | = passed ball |
| BK | = balk |

**6-3**

◀◀ The batter hit a ground ball to the shortstop (6), who then threw to first base (3) for the out.

**WP    =**

**E4**

◀◀ The batter hit a double. Then a wild pitch (WP) sent the runner to third. An error by the second baseman (E4) let the run score (triangle).

**PB    SB**

**E4**

◀◀ This batter reached first base on the second baseman's error. He then stole second (SB) and reached third on a passed ball.

**5-4**

**BB**

◀◀ After walking (BB), the runner was erased at second after the next batter (not shown) grounded to third. The third baseman (5) threw to second (4) for the force out.

# GOLD GLOVE
## RECORDS

Since 1957, the top fielders in each league have been given gold-plated Rawlings baseball gloves: the Gold Glove Award. These metal trophies wouldn't help catch baseballs, but these guys are so good in the field . . . who knows? Here are the players who have won the most Gold Gloves at each position.

**PITCHER**
- **18** Greg **Maddux**
- **16** Jim **Kaat**

**CATCHER**
- **13** Ivan **Rodriguez***
- **10** Johnny **Bench**

**FIRST BASE**
- **11** Keith **Hernandez**
- **9** Don **Mattingly**

**SECOND BASE**
- **10** Roberto **Alomar**
- **9** Ryne **Sandberg**

**THIRD BASE**
- **16** Brooks **Robinson**
- **10** Mike **Schmidt**

**SHORTSTOP**
- **13** Ozzie **Smith**
- **11** Omar **Vizquel**

**OUTFIELD**
- **12** Roberto **Clemente** ▶
- **12** Willie **Mays**
- **10** Ken **Griffey Jr.***
- **10** Andruw **Jones***
- **10** Al **Kaline**

*active player in 2009

# THE CATCH
## . . . AND OTHER FAMOUS DEFENSIVE PLAYS

Today's sports fans demand their Web Gems! That's what ESPN calls its rundown of the day's most spectacular defensive plays. Here's a look back at some of the most famous and amazing Web Gems in baseball history.

**A Wise Move** On July 23, 2009, Mark Buehrle of the White Sox pitched a perfect game (see page 67). But he wouldn't have without an amazing catch by center fielder Dewayne Wise. Wise raced to the fence, leaped, and snagged Gabe Kapler's drive before it could reach the seats. As Wise tumbled to the ground, the ball popped out of his glove . . . and he snagged it with his other hand!

**Jeter, Part I** In the 12th inning of a 2004 game, Yankees shortstop Derek Jeter tumbled into the seats to catch a foul pop. He climbed out with a bloody nose . . . and the ball.

**Jeter, Part II** That man again: During a 2001 AL divisional playoff game, Jeter tracked down a bad throw from the outfield and flipped the ball to catcher Jorge Posada, who tagged out the potential tying run. Jeter made the toss from near the first-base line!

**Edmonds Lays Out** The greatest catch ever? With his back to home plate, Jim Edmonds of the Angels dove, caught the ball, and skidded to the warning track in a 1997 game.

**Puckett's Game Saver** It wasn't the best catch ever, but the timing was perfect. In Game 6 of the 1991 World Series, Kirby Puckett of the Twins rose high against the left-field wall in Minnesota to keep Ron Gant's drive in the house. In the 11th inning, no one could catch Kirby's game-winning homer.

**The Wizard's Greatest Trick** This whole section could be about the amazing Ozzie Smith. "The Wizard of Oz" was perhaps the best infielder of all time. What many point to as his most memorable play came in 1978, when he was with the Padres. Diving behind second base for a ground ball, he had to shoot up his hand at the last second to snag a bad hop. He bounced up like a rubber ball and threw the runner out at first.

**Robinson Shuts Down the Machine** In the 1970 World Series, Brooks Robinson of the Orioles showed why he would win 16 Gold Gloves at third base. On several occasions—most memorably on Lee May's smash down the line—Robinson shut down the Big Red Machine with diving stops.

**The Catch** This one is so famous, you've probably seen it. In the 1954 World Series, Willie Mays of the Giants made an over-the-shoulder catch of a long drive by Cleveland's Vic Wertz. Mays did this about 450 feet from home plate, running full speed toward the wall. He then turned and fired the ball in so quickly that the baserunners could not even tag up.

## UNASSISTED TRIPLE PLAYS

One player, three outs: It's baseball's rarest defensive gem. An unassisted triple play happens when a single defensive player records all three outs on one batted ball.

For example, in 2009, the Phillies' Eric Bruntlett was playing second base. There were no outs and the Mets had runners on first and second. Bruntlett caught a line drive for the first out. He tagged second base to double off one runner for the second out. Then he tagged the runner coming from first for the third out. One player, three outs. Amazing. Here are the players who've made unassisted triple plays in the past 50 years. (Another seven occurred between 1909 and 1927.)

| PLAYER, TEAM | POSITION | YEAR |
|---|---|---|
| **Eric Bruntlett**, Phillies | 2B | 2009 |
| **Asdrubal Cabrera**, Indians | 2B | 2008 |
| **Troy Tulowitzki**, Rockies | SS | 2007 |
| **Rafael Furcal**, Dodgers | SS | 2003 |
| **Randy Velarde**, Athletics | 2B | 2000 |
| **John Valentin**, Red Sox | SS | 1994 |
| **Mickey Morandini**, Phillies | 2B | 1992 |
| **Ron Hansen**, Senators | SS | 1968 |

# THE *ULTIMATE* NINE

This is one of those argument-starters. Every baseball fan has his or her opinion on who is the "greatest" in all sorts of categories. But since this is my book, I get to pick first. Here are my choices for the best ever at each position. This is for defense only. A player's offensive and baserunning skills were not considered. Players are listed with the teams they played for the longest.

**CF** Ken GRIFFEY Jr.
Mariners/Reds

**LF** Barry BONDS
Pirates/Giants

**RF** Roberto CLEMENTE
Pirates

**SS** Ozzie SMITH
Cardinals

**2B** Bill MAZEROSKI
Pirates

**3B** Brooks ROBINSON
Orioles

**1B** Keith HERNANDEZ
Cardinals/Mets

**P** Greg MADDUX
Cubs/Braves

**C** Ivan RODRIGUEZ
Rangers

# KEY
# DEFENSIVE SKILLS

Every player has to be able to field ground balls, catch fly balls, and throw accurately. But there are other, more specialized defensive skills that come up in many games. Here's a look at a few of them:

**BLOCK THE PLATE:** Catchers put their bodies on the line to prevent baserunners from reaching the plate. The runners know this and can smash into the catcher like a linebacker in football.

**CHARGE BUNTS:** First and third basemen sprint toward home when they see a batter "square" to bunt. Fielders might grab the ball barehanded to throw the runner out in time.

**GO DEEP IN THE HOLE:** The hole is the space on the grass between short and third. Shortstops must range into this space to cut off grounders and then make the long throw to first.

**HIT THE CUTOFF MAN:** Outfielders remember this rule from their Little League days: Never overthrow the cutoff man! This infielder will relay the ball to the proper base.

**PICK OFF A RUNNER:** Pitchers, and sometimes catchers, throw to the bases to try to catch baserunners napping. Infielders have to be in position to make the catch and then the tag.

**SCOOP IT OUT:** First basemen snatch low throws out of the dirt with their big mitts. Other infielders say "Thanks!" for preventing a throwing error.

**TURN A DOUBLE PLAY:** It's a bit like ballet, as a middle infielder has to catch the ball, touch second base, leap over a sliding runner, and throw to beat the runner who is charging toward first base.

# THEFT KINGS

When you're playing baseball, it's okay to steal—bases, that is. The importance of the stolen base has declined recently. In the early years of baseball, stolen bases were a huge part of the game. (If we included pre-1900 players in these lists, they would dominate the page!) In the 1970s and 1980s, the steal came back big time, thanks to stars such as Rickey Henderson, Tim Raines, and Vince Coleman. These days, only a few players rack up even 50 steals in a season, a far cry from the all-time bests.

## MOST CAREER STOLEN BASES

| STOLEN BASES | PLAYER, YEARS |
| --- | --- |
| 1,406 | **Rickey Henderson**, 1979–2003 |
| 938 | **Lou Brock**, 1961–1979 |
| 892 | **Ty Cobb**, 1905–1928 |
| 808 | **Tim Raines**, 1979–1999, 2001–02 |
| 752 | **Vince Coleman**, 1985–1997 |

## MOST STOLEN BASES IN A SEASON

| STOLEN BASES | PLAYER, YEAR |
| --- | --- |
| 130 | **Rickey Henderson**, 1982 |
| 118 | **Lou Brock**, 1974 |
| 110 | **Vince Coleman**, 1985 |
| 109 | **Vince Coleman**, 1987 |
| 108 | **Rickey Henderson**, 1983 |

# HERO TIME

## Rickey Henderson

**By some measures,** Rickey Henderson just might be the best baseball player of all time. If you say that a player's main job is to score runs, then Henderson is the best, hands down. His career total of 2,295 is the most ever! If you say that a player's job is to get on base, then Henderson's right up there, too, with a career OBP of .401. If you look at a player's ability to stamp his influence on games, Henderson did a good job as well. He led off the game with a home run a record 81 times.

Playing for nine teams in his 25-year Hall of Fame career (most often for the Athletics and Yankees), Henderson electrified fans—and terrified opponents—with his speed. He would steal anywhere, anytime. When he was on base, the whole game changed. Pitchers got distracted, catchers got nervous, and infielders worried. Undoubtedly the greatest leadoff hitter of all time, his record of 1,406 stolen bases—more than 400 more than the second-place player—might never be topped.

# CHICAGO CUBS

The "Cubbies" are baseball's lovable losers. They haven't won a World Series since 1908! Yet their fans around the country remain loyal and loud. The Cubs have come close lately. Will this be their year . . . finally?

## GAME 1?
## 1876

The Cubs have been part of Chicago baseball since the days of President Ulysses S. Grant! They started out as the White Stockings, however.

 ## MAGIC MOMENT
### 1908 World Series

It's hard to believe, but the team's high point came more than 100 years ago, when it won its second straight title.

 ## LOWEST LOW
### 1984 NLCS

So many to choose from, but we'll go with this series, when the Cubs lost three straight after being up two games to none!

## STUFF

HOME:
**Wrigley Field**

WORLD SERIES TITLES: **2**

ONLY IN CHICAGO:
**Fans can sit on rooftop bleachers outside the ballpark and have a perfect view of the field.**

## STAR SEASONS!

**1907** The Cubs were champs for the first time! Pitcher "Three-Finger" Brown won the clincher.

**1984** Fan favorite Ryne "Ryno" Sandberg hit 19 triples and was named the NL MVP.

**1992** Greg Maddux won 20 games and the first of four straight NL Cy Young awards. Typical Cubs: He won the next three while pitching for Atlanta.

## The Ultimate Cub
# ERNIE BANKS

When your nickname is "Mr. Cub," you are also the *Ultimate* Cub. This Hall of Fame infielder was a powerful hitter (512 career homers), a two-time NL MVP, and one of the game's most energetic and positive ambassadors. "It's a nice day," he said. "Let's play two!"

**#1**

# FUNKY FACTS

→ The team was also known as the White Stockings, the Colts, and the Orphans. They've been the Cubs since 1903.

→ Wrigley Field facts: The ivy on the outfield walls was added in 1937. The ballpark didn't have lights until 1988.

→ Is there a "Billy Goat Curse"? In 1945, a man tried to bring a goat into a World Series game at Wrigley. He was kicked out, so he put a curse on the team. The Cubs haven't been to the World Series since!

→ Poor Steve Bartman. He was just a fan looking for a souvenir when he tried to catch a foul ball late in a 2003 playoff game that the Cubs led. Unfortunately,

## SUPERSTAR!
# GEOVANY SOTO

*This young catcher handles a solid Cubs pitching staff. Soto was named the NL Rookie of the Year in 2008 after blasting 23 homers. He's also a fine defensive catcher.*

Cubs left fielder Moises Alou was also trying to catch the high pop, and Bartman made him miss. The Cubs went on to lose the game and the series.

**You Can Look It Up!** CHICAGO'S OFFICIAL WEBSITE: www.chicagocubs.com

# CINCINNATI REDS

Pro baseball was born in Cincinnati in 1869. (See page 12.) From that undefeated squad to the 1970s Big Red Machine, the Reds have fielded some of the top teams of all time! But in recent years, they've been pretty bad.

## GAME 1? 1869

The Red Stockings were part of the original NL in 1876. Then they were kicked out of the league in 1880 because they sold beer and played on Sundays. They rejoined in 1890.

 ## MAGIC MOMENT
### 1975 World Series

In what some experts still call the best World Series ever, the Reds outlasted the Boston Red Sox in seven exciting games.

 ## LOWEST LOW
### Record Losses

For the only time in their long and storied history, the Reds lost more than 100 games (101, to be exact) in 1982.

## STUFF

**HOME:**
**Great American Ball Park**

**WORLD SERIES TITLES: 5**

**ONLY IN CINCINNATI:**
On those muggy summer days in Cincy, fans cool off by walking through misters in the stands.

## STAR SEASONS!

**1976** After the thrills of 1975, the Big Red Machine kept chugging, sweeping the Yankees for its second straight title.

**1988** Tom Browning threw a perfect game against the Dodgers, the team that would go on to win the World Series.

**1990** Pitcher Jose Rijo won two games in the Reds' World Series sweep of Oakland.

## The Ultimate Red
# PETE ROSE

In 19 years with the Reds, "Charlie Hustle" won three batting titles and led the NL in hits six times. He was the 1963 Rookie of the Year and the 1973 MVP. He also had 4,256 hits, the most ever. He later managed the team for six years. However, as the manager, he bet on the Reds. This was against baseball rules, and he was banned from the game. He's ineligible for the Hall of Fame.

# FUNKY FACTS

→ Way to go, kid! In 1944, 15-year-old Joe Nuxhall became the youngest major leaguer in history when pitched in a game for the Reds, whose roster had been depleted by World War II. He returned full-time in 1952.

→ Baseball's first night game was played in Cincinnati's Crosley Field in 1935 between the Reds and Phillies.

→ In 1938, the Reds' Johnny Vander Meer became the only pitcher to throw no-hitters in back-to-back starts.

## SUPERSTAR!
# JOEY VOTTO

The Reds are short on big-name superstars at the moment, but this young first baseman has the tools to become a top player. He's been a key RBI man for the club since he got a full-time job in 2008.

→ In the anti-Soviet Union 1950s, the team didn't want to be associated with Reds, the nickname of the United States' rival. So from 1954–1959, Cincinnati's team officially was called the Redlegs.

→ Cincy fans "stuffed" the ballot box for the 1957 All-Star Game, voting Redlegs players into seven starting spots! As a result, baseball (temporarily) stripped fans of their right to vote for the All-Star team!

**You Can Look It Up!** CINCINNATI'S OFFICIAL WEBSITE: www.cincinnatireds.com

# HOUSTON ASTROS

They're named for the astronauts who blast out of this world, but the Astros are without a championship here on Earth. They had some great teams in the late 1990s and early 2000s, but they're still awaiting liftoff!

## GAME 1?
## 1962

The team was originally called the Colt .45s, after a frontier-era pistol. When the team moved to the Astrodome in 1965, they changed their name to Astros.

 ## MAGIC MOMENT
### 2005 World Series

The Astros are still waiting for their first championship, though they did win the NL pennant this season. They lost the Series.

 ## LOWEST LOW
### Slow Start

Houston never finished higher than eighth in the NL in its first seven seasons. The low point was a 10th-place finish in 1968.

## STUFF

HOME:
**Minute Maid Park**

WORLD SERIES TITLES: **0**

ONLY IN HOUSTON:
**Built next to a train depot, Union Station, Minute Maid has a small train that circles part of the stadium.**

## STAR SEASONS!

**1981** Nolan Ryan mowed down the Dodgers for the fifth of his record seven no-hitters.

**1986** Mike Scott won the NL Cy Young Award, but the team fell two wins short of making the World Series.

**1991** First baseman Jeff Bagwell was named the NL Rookie of the Year, starting a great 15-year career in Houston.

## The Ultimate Astro
# CRAIG BIGGIO

With 3,060 hits, all as an Astro, Biggio is a surefire Hall of Famer. He's the majors' all-time leader in being hit by pitches and ranks fifth all-time in doubles. Biggio was very versatile, too. He started as a catcher in 1988 but later became an All-Star second baseman, while playing some outfield, too.

# FUNKY FACTS

➜ One of the early Houston sluggers was Jimmy "The Toy Cannon" Wynn, a good nickname for a player on a team then named for a gun.

➜ Over the years, the Astros have had some great sluggers, such as Jeff Bagwell, Lance Berkman, Jimmy Wynn, and Glenn Davis. So it's odd that they've never had a player lead the NL in homers.

➜ Until 2000, the Astros played indoors in the famous Houston Astrodome. But if they played indoors, how did a 1976 game against the Pittsburgh Pirates get rained out? Because a huge rainstorm flooded the streets and made it impossible for anyone to get to the ballpark!

## SUPERSTAR!
# HUNTER PENCE

He wears his socks pulled high, old-fashioned style, and Pence hustles like an old-time player, too. A fine outfielder, he has home-run power and a career average of nearly .300.

➜ The Astros boasted a lineup in the mid-1990s that featured the "Killer Bs," star players whose last names all began with B. Jeff Bagwell was joined by Lance Berkman, Craig Biggio, and others.

**You Can Look It Up!** HOUSTON'S OFFICIAL WEBSITE: www.houstonastros.com

# MILWAUKEE BREWERS

The city of Milwaukee has a long tradition of baseball. Its current team has not added many memorable seasons to that tradition. However, the Brewers have some top sluggers and are on the edge of greatness.

## GAME 1?
## 1969

The team played one unsuccessful season in Seattle as the expansion Pilots, before leaving the rainy Northwest for the chilly Midwest in 1970 (see Funky Facts for more).

 ## MAGIC MOMENT
### 1982 World Series

The Brewers' high point came when they were in the AL and won their only league pennant. They lost the Series to St. Louis.

 ## LOWEST LOW
### Bottom One

The team has been in the division cellar in one league or the other several times, but its worst season was 2002: 106 losses.

## STUFF

HOME:
**Miller Park**

WORLD SERIES TITLES: **0**

ONLY IN MILWAUKEE:
**At each game, fans watch people in giant sausage costumes race around the edge of the field. Really.**

## STAR SEASONS!

**1979** Part of a homer-happy team known as "Harvey's Wallbangers," Gorman Thomas led the AL with 45 dingers.

**1981** Double dip: Future Hall of Famer Rollie Fingers won the AL Cy Young and MVP awards with 28 saves and a 1.04 ERA.

**2004** Speedy outfielder Scott Podsednik led the NL with 70 stolen bases.

# The Ultimate Brewer
# ROBIN YOUNT

It takes a special player to earn an MVP award. So how special is a guy who wins two MVP awards . . . while playing two different positions! Robin Yount was a standout short-stop and the 1982 AL MVP. By 1989, he had moved to center field—and he won the award again! The Hall of Famer finished his career with 3,142 hits.

# FUNKY FACTS

➜ The great Hank Aaron spent his last two years (1975 and 1976) as a Brewer.

➜ The Milwaukee mascot is Bernie Brewer, who zips down a slide above the outfield wall whenever the Brewers hit a homer.

➜ During a sausage race (see Stuff box) in 2003, Pittsburgh's Randall Simon whacked the Italian sausage with his bat. It cost Simon a lot of sausages—he was arrested and fined, and the league suspended him for three games.

➜ The Brew Crew has been all over the majors. They played their first three seasons in the AL West, before moving to the

## SUPERSTAR!
# PRINCE FIELDER

Hey, kids, eat your veggies! Prince Fielder is one of base-ball's strongest sluggers. He had 50 homers in 2007 and 30-plus in two other seasons. Why the food note? Fielder is a vegetarian!

AL East for 22 years. After a short, four-year stretch in the AL Central, they left the American League entirely. They've played in the NL Central since 1998.

**You Can Look It Up!** MILWAUKEE'S OFFICIAL WEBSITE: www.milwaukeebrewers.com

# PITTSBURGH PIRATES

One of the oldest teams in baseball, the Pirates have, sadly, also been one of the worst for quite a long time. They always seem to lose their young stars to other teams, but hope springs eternal in the Steel City.

## GAME 1?
## 1882

The Alleghenies were one of the American Association's original teams. They switched to the National League in 1887. In 1891, they changed their name to the Pirates.

##  MAGIC MOMENT
### 1960 World Series

With a Series-winning home run in the bottom of the ninth in Game 7, Bill Mazeroski set off a celebration at home plate.

##  LOWEST LOW
### So Many Choices

With more than a dozen last-place finishes to choose from, we'll go with the 112-loss 1952 team as the lowest of the low.

## STUFF

HOME:
**PNC Park**

WORLD SERIES TITLES: **5**

ONLY IN PITTSBURGH:
**A ballpark exhibit including statues and posters honors the city's famed Negro League teams and players.**

## STAR SEASONS!

**1925** The Pirates overcame Hall of Fame pitcher Walter Johnson to capture their second World Series title.

**1979** The "We Are Family" Pirates, named for a popular song, stormed to a World Series title.

**1992** The Pirates earned their third straight trip to the NLCS— and lost that playoff series for the third straight time.

## The Ultimate Pirate
# HONUS WAGNER

"The Dutchman" played his last game in 1917, but he's still regarded as one of the best shortstops of all time. An eight-time NL batting champ, Wagner was also the all-time leader in steals until Ty Cobb topped him. Wagner also helped the Pirates win their first World Series.

**#1**

# FUNKY FACTS

→ The team became the Pirates after "stealing" star Louis Bierbauer from the rival Philadelphia Athletics in 1891.

→ Puerto Rico's Roberto Clemente was the first great major leaguer from Latin America. He starred for the Pirates for 18 seasons, finishing with a record 12 Gold Gloves in the outfield and 3,000 hits.

→ Ralph Kiner led the NL with 37 homers for the 1952 Pirates, but the team finished in eighth place (out of eight teams). He asked for a raise. The boss said no. "We finished last with you," the boss said. "We can finish last without you."

## SUPERSTAR!
# ANDREW McCUTCHEN

*This young center fielder might be the centerpiece for Pittsburgh for a long time. With great speed, he's a fantastic outfielder and baserunner, and he's shown flashes of power at the plate.*

→ The team mascot is a giant, green, bird-like thing called the Pirate Parrot. No, he doesn't stand on someone's shoulder the whole game.

**You Can Look It Up!** PITTSBURGH'S OFFICIAL WEBSITE: www.pittsburghpirates.com

# ST. LOUIS
# CARDINALS

You might say that the Cardinals are the Yankees of the National League. Only the Yanks have won more than the Cardinals' ten World Series titles. St. Louis is a great baseball town with more championships in its future.

## GAME 1?
## 1882

The team started out as the St. Louis Brown Stockings in the American Association. The name was soon shortened to the Browns, who joined the NL in 1892.

 **MAGIC MOMENT**
### 2006 World Series

All the Cards' titles have been special, but to win this one, they had to overcome being the playoff team with the worst record.

 **LOWEST LOW**
### Last Place in '90

This was the only last-place finish for the Cards since baseball went to a division format beginning in the 1969 season.

## STUFF

HOME:
**Busch Stadium**

WORLD SERIES TITLES: **10**

ONLY IN ST. LOUIS:
**Fans can make their own stuffed version of Fredbird, the team mascot, in a store inside Busch Stadium.**

## STAR SEASONS!

**1924** Rogers "The Rajah" Hornsby hit .424, the highest average by any 20th-century player.

**1937** Outfielder Joe Medwick won the Triple Crown, batting .324 with 31 home runs and 154 RBIs.

**2003** Albert Pujols led the NL with a .359 average. He also had the first of four straight 40-homer seasons.

## The Ultimate Cardinal
# STAN MUSIAL

Stan "The Man" Musial is one of the beloved figures in baseball, loved as much for his sunny and generous personality as for his hitting. The three-time MVP is the Cardinals' all-time leader in hits, runs, doubles, homers, games, at-bats, and RBIs. His 3,630 hits are the fourth-most in major league history.

# FUNKY FACTS

→ Before becoming the Cardinals in 1900, the team was the Brown Stockings, the Browns, and the Perfectos.

→ The 1934 Cardinals earned a famous team nickname thanks to their dirty uniforms and rough-and-tumble style. A New York writer named them for a grungy part of Manhattan, dubbing the Cardinals the "Gas House Gang."

→ St. Louis star Joe "Ducky" Medwick was chased off the field late in Game 7 of the 1934 World Series. Hometown Detroit Tigers fans threw garbage at him after he had slid hard into second base the inning before!

## SUPERSTAR!
# ALBERT PUJOLS

*Best player in baseball? That's easy. It's the Cardinals' power-hitting first baseman. He's won three MVP awards and finished in the top four of the voting five other times. Need a big hit? Call Pujols.*

→ How good was right-handed pitcher Bob Gibson? Thanks to him, they lowered the pitching mound. Gibson's 1.12 ERA in 1968 was the lowest in 54 years. Baseball took pity on hitters and lowered the mound by five inches in 1969.

**You Can Look It Up!** ST. LOUIS'S OFFICIAL WEBSITE: www.stlouiscardinals.com

1903
WORLD
SERIES
CHAMPIONS

1904

AMERICAN
LEAGUE
CHAMPIONS

# EXTRA INNINGS!

**Baseball is lots more** than pitching, hitting, and defense. There is a whole culture surrounding the game and its history. In this chapter, we'll take a look at a few aspects of that culture. From baseball language to funny nicknames, from trips to the minors to a visit with fabled Negro League players, this is our seventh-inning stretch of a chapter.

## INSIDE:

*Banners at Fenway Park celebrate past Red Sox titles.*

# BASEBALL SAYINGS

One awesome, 1,008-page baseball dictionary provides definitions for thousands of baseball-related expressions. Here are some of the phrases and sayings that you'll hear at the ballpark, on the radio, or from your friends in the "Hot Stove League." (That's what old-timers call the offseason; in the past, people would sit around the stove to stay warm and chat about baseball.)

## PHRASES

**back-to-back jack** home runs hit by a pair of teammates in consecutive at-bats

**Baltimore chop** a ball that bounces high into the air off the dirt in front of home plate

**can of corn** an easy fly ball

**cue shot** a ball hit off of the end of the bat

**dying quail** a bloop fly ball that barely gets out of the infield

**flashing the signs** when a coach uses hand signals to give instructions to batters and baserunners

**ins and outs** pregame infield and outfield practice

**kangaroo hop** a sudden and unexpected bounce taken by a batted ball

**keystone sack** second base

**on the black** pitches that zip over the edges of home plate

**pitcher's best friend** a double play

**pull the string** to fool the batter by throwing a slow pitch

**seeing-eye single** a ground ball that just barely eludes the infielders

## HOME RUNS
Other names for the "big fly":

* CIRCUIT CLOUT
* DINGER
* CUADRANGULAR (SPANISH)
* DOWNTOWN
* TATER
* TOUCH 'EM ALL
* YARD BALL

**step in the bucket** a batter moving his front foot away from home plate as he swings

**swing from the heels** to swing the bat as hard as possible, rather than take a controlled swing

**wheelhouse** the place where a batter can hit the ball best; usually down the middle of the strike zone

## SAYINGS

**He was really flashing the leather!** A saying that means a fielder was making many great catches.

**Hit the showers.** Said to an unsuccessful pitcher being taken out of a game.

**It just takes one!** Yelled by teammates when encouraging a batter to come through with a big hit.

**Pick him up!** Two meanings: coming through with a big hit after a teammate has either failed to do so or has made an error the previous inning. Also means to bring glove and hat out to a player who was stranded on the bases at the end of an inning.

**Take two and hit to right.** When you get two strikes, shorten your batting stroke and just try to poke the ball to the opposite field (right field since most hitters are right-handed).

**Way to take one for the team!** Yelled to players who get hit by a pitch, especially in a situation where it helps the team keep a big inning going.

*"pull the string"*

# BASEBALL
# NICKNAMES

Slugger George Herman Ruth probably had the most nicknames: Babe, Bambino, Sultan of Swat, Caliph of Clout, Wazir of Wham, etc. Ted Williams owned a few colorful ones: The Kid, Teddy Ballgame, the Splendid Splinter. In those old days, baseball was packed with great nicknames. Here's a look at some of the more interesting player (and team) nicknames from yesterday and today.

## PLAYERS

Dennis **"Oil Can"** Boyd

Bob **"Death to Flying Things"** Ferguson

Al **"The Mad Hungarian"** Hrabosky

Reggie Jackson, **"Mr. October"**

Bill **"Spaceman"** Lee

Pepper Martin, **"The Wild Horse of the Osage"**

Willie Mays, the **"Say-Hey Kid"**

Paul **"Big Poison"** Waner

Lloyd **"Little Poison"** Waner

## TEAMS

Angels: **The Halos**

Indians: **The Tribe**

Reds (1970s): **The Big Red Machine**

Red Sox: **Hub Hose** (Hub is a nickname for Boston)

White Sox: **Pale Hose**

Yankees: **Bronx Bombers**

# GIRLS' BASEBALL

In 1941, hundreds of major league baseball players headed off to fight in World War II. On the "home front," women played a much bigger role, taking on jobs previously performed by men. In 1943, Cubs owner William Wrigley started a league of female baseball players, the All-American Girls Professional Baseball League (AAGPBL). They played softball for the first two seasons, before switching to real baseball. The war ended in 1945, but the women's league played on until 1954.

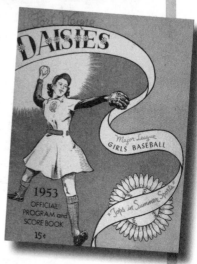

## AAGPBL Teams*

**Fort Wayne Daisies** (1945–1954)

**Grand Rapids Chicks**
(1945–1954)

**Kalamazoo Lassies** (1950–1954)

**Kenosha Comets** (1943–1951)

**Muskegon Lassies** (1946–1949)

**Peoria Redwings** (1946–1952)

**Racine Belles** (1943–1950)

**Rockford Peaches** (1943–1954)

**South Bend Blue Sox**
(1943–1954)

*These are the teams that played for at least three AAGPBL seasons.

## AAGPBL Champions

| | |
|---|---|
| 1943 | **Racine Belles** |
| 1944 | **Milwaukee Chicks** |
| 1945 | **Rockford Peaches** |
| 1946 | **Racine Belles** |
| 1947 | **Grand Rapids Chicks** |
| 1948 | **Rockford Peaches** |
| 1949 | **Rockford Peaches** |
| 1950 | **Rockford Peaches** |
| 1951 | **South Bend Blue Sox** |
| 1952 | **South Bend Blue Sox** |
| 1953 | **Grand Rapids Chicks** |
| 1954 | **Kalamazoo Lassies** |

# MINOR LEAGUE
## BASEBALL

Major League Baseball is not the only (pro) game in town. Since 1901, teams have played what's now called Minor League Baseball. Playing for "farm teams" in "the bush leagues" or simply "the minors," young players develop their skills in the hopes of working their way up to the majors. Since 1921, major league teams have owned and run minor league teams, creating "pipelines" to the "big clubs."

The years after World War II were the biggest for the minors, with 448 teams playing in 59 leagues. However, TV and expansion in the majors cut into the minors' audience. Today, minor league teams are still important to their local communities, while also serving as training grounds for future major leaguers. Major league games can be hard to get to and expensive, but minor league games are played in smaller, local parks with lower ticket prices. Check out a game sometime!

## MAJOR MOMENTS IN MINOR LEAGUES

### ◀◀ 1933: Joe's Other Streak

Joe DiMaggio would gain lasting fame for his 56-game hitting streak with the Yankees in 1941. But in 1933, he had an even longer streak—61 games!—while playing for the Pacific Coast League's San Francisco Seals, his hometown team.

### 1946: Robinson Debuts

Win a trivia contest by naming the team that Jackie Robinson played for to break the color line. It wasn't the Brooklyn Dodgers. Robinson made his debut this year with a Brooklyn Dodgers minor league team, the Montreal Royals.

## 1954: Bauman's Big Year

Joe Bauman hit 72 homers for the Roswell Rockets of New Mexico. This was the most in a single season in pro ball until Barry Bonds of the Giants topped him with 73 in 2004.

## 1981: Longest Game Ever

The Pawtucket Red Sox and the Rochester Red Wings needed 33 innings and parts of three days to finish the longest game in pro baseball history. Pawtucket finally won 3–2.

## 1983: First Female Ump (Sort of)

Pam Postema took the field in a Triple A game as an umpire. Bernice Gera had umped one game back in 1972, but Postema became the first full-time woman umpire.

## 1991: Most Fans Ever

The Buffalo Bison drew 1,240,951 fans this season to set an all-time record for minor league baseball.

## 2007: Is That Who I Think it Is?

Trenton Thunder fans saw a surprise start by seven-time Cy Young winner Roger Clemens, who was tuning up for the Yankees.

# THE MINOR LEAGUES

Major league clubs assign levels to their minor league teams. Here they are, ranked from highest to lowest.

**AAA** (Triple A)

**AA** (Double A)

**A** (Single A or A Ball)

**Advanced A**

**Short-Season A**

**Rookie**

# BEST MINOR NAMES

Minor league teams do all sorts of wacky things to get fans to come to games. One trick is to use odd nicknames. Here's a list of baseball team names. Eight of them are real; two are not. Can you spot the phonies?

Albuquerque Isotopes

Batavia Muckdogs

Border City Beef Patties

Everett AquaSox

Lehigh Valley IronPigs

Outer Valley Plum-Pickers

Rancho Cucamonga Quakes

Toledo Mud Hens

Tri-City Dust Devils

Vermont Lake Monsters

ANSWERS: Not Real: Border City Beef Patties, Outer Valley Plum-Pickers.

# BALLPARKS

They're ballparks, not stadiums. You play football in a stadium, you play baseball in a ballpark. We know, there's Yankee Stadium and Dodger Stadium and Busch Stadium, yadda, yadda, yadda. To this author, they'll always be ballparks. In the past decade, more than a dozen new "stadiums" have been built for major league teams. But most of them are designed to look like old-time, old-fashioned, cute-and-cozy . . . ballparks.

| OLDEST | NL: **WRIGLEY FIELD** ▲, Cubs, 1914* |
| | AL: **FENWAY PARK**, Red Sox, 1912 |
| NEWEST | NL: **CITI FIELD**, Mets, 2009 |
| | AL: **TARGET FIELD**, Twins, 2010 |
| BIGGEST** | NL: **DODGER STADIUM**, 56,000 |
| | AL: **YANKEE STADIUM**, 52,325 |
| SMALLEST** | NL: **PNC PARK**, Pirates, 38,496 |
| | AL: **OAKLAND COLISEUM**, Athletics, 35,067*** |
| RETRACTABLE ROOFS | NL: **ARIZONA, HOUSTON, MILWAUKEE** |
| | AL: **SEATTLE, TORONTO** |

*Cubs' first game there in 1916   **by number of seats   ***Can be expanded . . . but rarely is!

# 2010
# MAJOR LEAGUE
## BALLPARKS

Note: Many ballparks are named for sponsors, who pay for the naming rights. These sponsors change sometimes, so check www.mlb.com for the latest names.

| TEAM | BALLPARK NAME |
| --- | --- |
| Arizona Diamondbacks | **Chase Field** |
| Atlanta Braves | **Turner Field** |
| Baltimore Orioles | **Oriole Park at Camden Yards** |
| Boston Red Sox | **Fenway Park** |
| Chicago Cubs | **Wrigley Field** |
| Chicago White Sox | **U.S. Cellular Field** |
| Cincinnati Reds | **Great American Ball Park** |
| Cleveland Indians | **Progressive Field** |
| Colorado Rockies | **Coors Field** |
| Detroit Tigers | **Comerica Park** |
| Houston Astros | **Minute Maid Park** |
| Kansas City Royals | **Kauffman Stadium** |
| Los Angeles Angels of Anaheim | **Angel Stadium of Anaheim** |
| Los Angeles Dodgers | **Dodger Stadium** |
| Miami Marlins | **Land Shark Stadium** |
| Milwaukee Brewers | **Miller Park** |
| Minnesota Twins | **Target Field** |
| New York Mets | **Citi Field** |
| New York Yankees | **Yankee Stadium** |
| Oakland Athletics | **Oakland-Alameda County Coliseum** |
| Philadelphia Phillies | **Citizens Bank Park** |
| Pittsburgh Pirates | **PNC Park** |
| St. Louis Cardinals | **Busch Stadium** |
| San Diego Padres | **PETCO Park** |
| San Francisco Giants | **AT&T Park** |
| Seattle Mariners | **Safeco Field** |
| Tampa Bay Rays | **Tropicana Field** |
| Texas Rangers | **Rangers Ballpark in Arlington** |
| Toronto Blue Jays | **Rogers Centre** |
| Washington Nationals | **Nationals Park** |

# SHADOW BALL

## THE STORY OF THE NEGRO LEAGUES

**Can you imagine** baseball without Ryan Howard? Or without Ken Griffey Jr.? Or C.C. Sabathia? Or Prince Fielder? Had those players been born a few decades earlier, you might never have heard of them or seen their marvelous skills. Why not?

In 1884, Moses Fleetwood Walker played catcher for the Toledo team in the old American Association. After Walker, no African American players were allowed to play in any of the top pro leagues until 1947. But for all those decades, black athletes didn't let the bigotry and racism of big-league owners and fans stop them. They formed all-black teams that played one another.

In 1920, a former star pitcher named Rube Foster formed the Negro National League (NNL). In 1923, the Eastern Colored League began play. Black baseball was more organized than it had ever been before, but money problems caused both leagues to close by 1931.

The NNL was reborn in 1933 with new leaders, and the Negro American League was established in 1937. Now the Negro Leagues were in their prime. Stars such as Josh Gibson and Satchel Paige (see page 124), Cool Papa Bell and Oscar Charleston, Judy Johnson and Martin Dihigo excelled, attracting huge crowds of both

## NEGRO LEAGUE WORLD SERIES RESULTS

(NNL: Negro National League; NAL: Negro American League)

| Year | Winner | Runner-up |
|------|--------|-----------|
| 1942 | **KANSAS CITY MONARCHS** NAL | Homestead Grays NNL |
| 1943 | **HOMESTEAD GRAYS** NNL | Birmingham Black Barons NAL |
| 1944 | **HOMESTEAD GRAYS** NNL | Birmingham Black Barons NAL |
| 1945 | **CLEVELAND BUCKEYES** NAL | Homestead Grays NNL |
| 1946 | **NEWARK EAGLES** NNL | Kansas City Monarchs NAL |
| 1947 | **NEW YORK CUBANS** NNL | Cleveland Buckeyes NAL |
| 1948 | **HOMESTEAD GRAYS** NNL | Birmingham Black Barons NAL |

black and white fans. Black players also took part in some exhibition games against traveling teams made up of white major league stars.

The Negro League teams were enormously popular with black fans. In the divided world of America, stars like Gibson and Bell were as famous in their communities as Babe Ruth and Bob Feller were in theirs.

Another way for black players to hit the diamond was to leave the country. Leagues in Mexico and the Caribbean islands needed players, and they had no problem hiring African Americans. Many black players were stars in Cuba, Mexico, and the Dominican Republic.

In the 1940s, the top two Negro Leagues held an annual championship, their own World Series. Following World War II,

however, things changed. Many African Americans had fought and died for their country during the war. A feeling began to grow that it was wrong for them to be kept from the national game. On April 15, 1947, Branch Rickey of the Brooklyn Dodgers arranged for Jackie Robinson to play first base for his team, becoming the first African American in the 20th century to play in the majors. A terrible era was over. (The NFL and NBA had integrated around the same time.)

The move to the majors by top black players over the following decade meant the end of the Negro Leagues. By 1960, there were no all-black pro teams left. A sad chapter of American history had ended—but there was no sadness in the joy and skill that Negro League players brought to the game.

# HERO TIME

## Josh Gibson

**Some people say** he was the greatest power hitter of all time. Fans who saw him hit said he was more powerful than Babe Ruth and could crush homers out of the biggest ballparks. Players who faced him claimed he could throw out baserunners without ever leaving his crouch.

But catcher Josh Gibson never played a game in the major leagues. As an African American playing in the 1930s and 1940s, he was banned from the bigs. He was a star, however, in the Negro Leagues, playing mostly for the Pittsburgh Crawfords and the Homestead Grays.

Gibson's feats were legendary. It was said he crushed the longest homer ever hit at Washington's Griffith Stadium. His teams didn't keep

exact stats, but he's sometimes credited with more than 800 career homers (take that, Barry Bonds!). In games that he played against teams of white major leaguers, Gibson hit .426.

But Gibson struggled with drugs and alcohol and died when he was only 35 years old. Although he was one of baseball's greatest players, his story was one of its saddest. Josh Gibson was elected to the Baseball Hall of Fame in 1972.

# Satchel Paige

**A natural showman** as well as one of the finest pitchers of all time, Satchel Paige had one of baseball's longest careers. He made his mark on all-black teams (the Hall of Fame lists him on 12!), playing anytime, anywhere, all year round. In Negro League circles, he was the most feared and beloved pitcher.

When he was 42 in 1948, well past his prime, he joined the AL's Cleveland Indians. He later played with the NL's St. Louis Browns from 1951–1953 and made the All-Star Game twice. He even came back in 1965 at the age of 59 to pitch in a game for the Kansas City Athletics, making him the oldest player ever in the major leagues.

From the funny names he gave his pitches (the Be Ball, the Hesitation Pitch) to the stories about his exhibition games (he supposedly called his fielders in and then struck all three batters), Paige was one of a kind. In 1971, he was the first Negro League player elected to the Hall of Fame.

# ARIZONA
# DIAMONDBACKS

Like another expansion team, the Florida Marlins, the Diamondbacks earned a championship early in their history. They've brought regular-season baseball to a state that had normally only seen it during spring training!

## GAME 1?
## 1998

The Arizona expansion team was named after a poisonous local snake, but the owners liked the mix of Western wildlife with a nice little bit of baseball wordplay!

 ## MAGIC MOMENT
### Luis's Liner: 2001

Luis Gonzalez blooped an 11th-inning single off Mariano Rivera to make the D-Backs the fastest team to win a World Series title.

 ## LOWEST LOW
### Snakebitten

Arizona fell into the Grand Canyon in 2004, losing 111 games for one of the worst seasons in recent NL history.

## STUFF

HOME:
**Chase Field**

WORLD SERIES TITLES: **1**

ONLY IN PHOENIX:
**To help fans combat the desert heat when the retractable roof is open, the ballpark has a swimming pool behind right field.**

## STAR SEASONS!

**1999** Speedy Tony Womack helped the D-backs reach 100 wins in their second season by leading the NL with 72 stolen bases.

**2001** Luis Gonzalez set an Arizona team record by slugging a career-best 57 homers.

**2006** Brandon Webb won the NL Cy Young Award with 16 wins and a 3.10 ERA.

The Ultimate Diamondback

# RANDY JOHNSON

Although he only played eight years in Arizona during what will surely be a Hall of Fame career, Johnson is the team leader in wins and ERA. He won four straight Cy Young awards (1999–2002) with Arizona, plus helped the team win the World Series in 2001, when he was the Series co-MVP.

**#1**

# FUNKY FACTS

➔ When Arizona's owners needed a name for their new team, they just looked to the desert. Before they settled on Diamondbacks, they considered Coyotes and Scorpions.

➔ Having a costumed snake as a mascot would be tough. How would it sign autographs or throw T-shirts into the stands? So to give its mascot some hands, er, paws, Arizona created Baxter the Bobcat.

➔ On May 18, 2004, Randy Johnson (see Ultimate Diamondback above) became the 17th and, at 40 years old, the oldest pitcher to throw a perfect game. He beat the Atlanta Braves 2–0 to join this elite group of perfect pitchers.

SUPERSTAR!

# BRANDON WEBB

Continuing Arizona's tradition of great starting pitching, Webb's power sinker has made him one of the NL's most feared hurlers. The 2006 Cy Young winner has twice led the NL in wins.

➔ The first teams to hold spring training in Arizona were the Cleveland Indians and the then-New York Giants, who both made the trip in 1946.

**You Can Look It Up!** ARIZONA'S OFFICIAL WEBSITE: www.diamondbacks.com

# COLORADO ROCKIES

Few expansion teams have gotten as much instant support as the Rockies. They set the major league attendance record (4,483,350) in 1993 and have topped three million eight other times. Rocky Mountain Happy!

## GAME 1?
## 1993

Some experts didn't think a team could succeed at Denver's mile-high altitude. But fans loved the offensive firepower of early Rockies teams, and baseball's here to stay in Colorado.

 ## MAGIC MOMENT
### 2007 World Series

The Rockies won 20 of 21 games to make the playoffs and then reach the World Series. But they lost to Boston in four games.

 ## LOWEST LOW
### Tumblin' Rockies

Colorado has never had a really bad team, but in 2005, the Rockies did finish last in the NL West with 95 losses.

## STUFF

HOME:
**Coors Field**

WORLD SERIES TITLES: **0**

ONLY IN DENVER:
**Sit in the special purple seats in Row 20 of the upper deck, and you'll find yourself exactly one mile above sea level.**

## STAR SEASONS!

**1995** Did the thin air help? Dante Bichette's 40 homers led the NL, the first of three straight seasons a Rockies player topped that category.

**1996** Andres "The Big Cat" Galarraga led the NL with 47 homers and 150 RBIs.

**1999** Larry Walker won the NL batting title with a .379 average, still the highest since 1994.

## The Ultimate Rockie
# LARRY WALKER

Although he was already a top hitter when he joined Colorado in 1995, he got even better with the Rockies, winning three NL batting titles, five Gold Gloves, and the 1997 NL MVP award. Walker was perhaps the best overall player ever from Canada.

**#1**

# FUNKY FACTS

➔ Baseballs fly farther and faster in the thin, dry air of mile-high Denver. To reduce the impact of the altitude on their games, the Rockies began storing their baseballs in a humidor. This humidity-controlled room makes the baseballs respond as if they were at sea level.

➔ The Rockies mascot is NOT a giant rock. That would be boring. Instead, the team turned to Colorado's history of fossil findings to create Dinger, a purple triceratops. Where'd the name come from? It's a nickname for a home run. Colorado hits them in bunches.

## SUPERSTAR!
# TODD HELTON

*Helton is perhaps the least-known superstar hitter in baseball. In 13 seasons with Colorado, he has one of the best career slugging averages ever, six 30-homer seasons, and a batting average of .328.*

➔ Outfielder Ryan Spilborghs is one of five major leaguers who wear No. 19 to honor their former summer-ball coach Eric Pintard, who passed away from cancer in 2004. Before he died, Pintard started a baseball charity that helps kids with cancer.

**You Can Look It Up!** COLORADO'S OFFICIAL WEBSITE: www.coloradorockies.com

# LOS ANGELES
# DODGERS

The Dodgers made history twice. In 1947, they played the first African American major leaguer in the 1900s, Jackie Robinson. (See page 45.) In 1958, they became one of the first two teams to move to the West Coast.

## GAME 1?
## 1884

Why Dodgers? Brooklynites often had to avoid streetcars called trolleys. Locals called themselves "Trolley-Dodgers." The team grabbed the shortened nickname in 1911.

##  MAGIC MOMENT
### 1955 World Series

Fans in Brooklyn always shouted, "Wait 'til next year," as the Dodgers lost seven World Series. Finally, 1955 was their year.

## LOWEST LOW
### Bottom Rung

Since divisional play started in 1969, the Dodgers have finished last in the NL West just once, with 99 losses in 1992.

## STUFF

**HOME:**
**Dodger Stadium**

WORLD SERIES TITLES: **6**

ONLY IN LA:
**Fans who sit in the right-field bleachers get all the hot dogs, nachos, and peanuts they can eat—all for the price of the seat.**

## STAR SEASONS!

**1956** Don Newcombe won the first Cy Young Award and was also named the NL MVP.

**1965** Sandy Koufax threw a perfect game against the Cubs. It was his then-record fourth no-hitter. He also won the second of his three Cy Young awards.

**1997** Mike Piazza set an NL record for highest batting average by a catcher at .362.

# The Ultimate Dodger
# VIN SCULLY

This was a tough one, since the team has had so many stars in its two homes. But one voice has been with them for more than 50 years: Hall of Fame play-by-play announcer Vin Scully. Generations of Dodgers fans grew up listening to him, either in Brooklyn or after the team moved to LA.

**#1**

# FUNKY FACTS

➔ Among this team's pre-Dodgers nicknames: Atlantics, Bridegrooms, Superbas, and Robins.

➔ Rick Monday's greatest moment in baseball came between pitches. In 1976, the outfielder snatched an American flag away from protesters who were trying to light it after running onto the field.

➔ Start 'em young: The Dodgers had five straight NL Rookies of the Year (1992–1996): Eric Karros, Mike Piazza, Raul Mondesi, Hideo Nomo, and Todd Hollandsworth.

➔ Slugger Manny Ramirez knows how to be dramatic.

## SUPERSTAR!
# ANDRE ETHIER

*This hot-hitting outfielder is one of several young stars who have turned the Dodgers into an NL powerhouse. Ethier won six games in 2009 with "walk-off" RBI hits.*

In 2009, on Manny Ramirez Bobblehead Night, he came off the bench to pinch-hit with an injured hand . . . and hit a grand slam that won the game!

**You Can Look It Up!** LOS ANGELES'S OFFICIAL WEBSITE: www.dodgers.com

# SAN DIEGO PADRES

With all the baseball stars playing in California, the Padres haven't gotten as much attention as the mighty Dodgers, the fun-loving A's, or the venerable Giants. But they've given their fans some pretty good times in SD.

## GAME 1?
## 1969

California got its fifth major league team with baseball's 1969 expansion. Padres fans are still waiting for their first World Series, but who minds hanging out in this great weather?

 ## MAGIC MOMENT
### 1984 NLCS

Down two games to none to the Chicago Cubs, the Padres roared back to win three straight and take the NL pennant.

 ## LOWEST LOW
### A Slow Start

The Padres finished last in the NL West in each of their first six seasons, losing 100 or more games four times.

## STUFF

HOME:
**PETCO Park**

WORLD SERIES TITLES: **0**

ONLY IN SAN DIEGO:
**At the "Park at the Park," fans can relax on the grass and take in Padres games from beyond the outfield fence.**

## STAR SEASONS!

**1976** Randy Jones won 22 games and the Padres' first NL Cy Young Award.

**1994** In a season that was cut short by a strike, Tony Gwynn flirted with .400, ending the season at a stunning .394.

**2006** Closer Trevor Hoffman set the all-time record for saves with his 479th, topping the record set by Lee Smith.

## The Ultimate Padre
# TONY GWYNN

With eight NL batting titles, Gwynn was one of the best pure hitters in history. In 20 seasons, he became San Diego's all-time leader in batting average, hits, runs, games played, RBIs, and total bases. A rare superstar who spent his whole career with one team, Gwynn is Mr. Padre.

**#1**

# FUNKY FACTS

➜ There was once a minor league San Diego Padres team. It played in the Pacific Coast League from 1936–1968. Several of its players went on to become major league stars, including the great Ted Williams.

➜ The Padres' official mascot is the Swinging Friar, but the Famous Chicken is more, um, famous. The Famous Chicken was known as the San Diego Chicken when he first appeared at Padres games in the late 1970s. He later flew the coop to become a national star.

➜ In 1974, the Padres almost moved to Washington, D.C. But

## SUPERSTAR!
# ADRIAN GONZALEZ

*Gonzalez's home-run power erupted in 2009, as he led the team's offense. His heritage also makes him a popular figure with San Diego's large Mexican population.*

Ray Kroc bought the team and kept it in San Diego. Kroc knew about running a business: He was the owner of McDonald's.

➜ Before a switch to blue and white in 2004, the team uniform was mainly brown. Yuck!

**You Can Look It Up!** SAN DIEGO'S OFFICIAL WEBSITE: www.sandiegopadres.com

# SAN FRANCISCO GIANTS

The Giants are one of the two teams, along with the Dodgers, that brought baseball west. They played in New York City until moving to San Francisco in 1958. They've been one of the most successful NL teams.

## GAME 1?
## 1883

The team joined the NL in 1883 as the Gothams, a nickname for New York City (and yes, that's where Batman's hometown got its name). They became the Giants in 1885.

 ## MAGIC MOMENT
### The Catch

Big underdogs to the Indians, the Giants won the 1954 World Series, inspired by Willie Mays's miraculous catch in Game 1.

 ## LOWEST LOW
### One Bad Year

In 126 seasons, the Giants have lost 100 games only once. They lost exactly that number in 1985. They finished last, of course.

## STUFF

HOME:
**AT&T Park**

WORLD SERIES TITLES: **5**

ONLY IN SAN FRANCISCO:
**Fans can paddle their kayaks into McCovey Cove behind right field and try to snag homers that fly over the wall.**

## STAR SEASONS!

**1905** Star pitcher Christy Mathewson threw three shutouts in six days, and the Giants won their first World Series.

**1969** The great Juan Marichal used his famous high-kick delivery to lead the NL with a 2.10 ERA.

**2001** Slugger Barry Bonds smashed the single-season homer record with 73 in 2001.

## The Ultimate Giant
# WILLIE MAYS

Some experts call the "Say-Hey Kid" the best all-around player of all time. Power? He hit 660 homers. Speed? He led the NL in steals four times. Defense? He was probably the best center fielder ever and won 12 Gold Gloves. Clutch? His catch in the 1954 Series turned the tide in favor of his team. He's a giant among Giants.

# FUNKY FACTS

➔ The first World Series was in 1903. The second wasn't until 1905. That's because the 1904 NL-champion Giants refused to play the AL champs, whom they considered inferior!

➔ The Giants' old home in Candlestick Park was famously windy. In one game, pitcher Stu Miller was blown off the mound by a strong gust of wind.

➔ The Giants created one of the worst mascots of all time—on purpose! The Crazy Crab debuted as a joke in 1984. It worked; the fans booed and the crustacean's goofy antics doomed it to a quick exit.

➔ Giants right-hander Gaylord Perry tossed a no-hitter against

## SUPERSTAR!
# TIM LINCECUM

*He looks like he's about 15, but he pitches like a veteran. Lincecum's odd motion and great arm have helped him win the 2008 and 2009 NL Cy Young awards and lead the league in strikeouts twice.*

the St. Louis Cardinals in 1968, winning 1–0 on September 17 at Candlestick Park. The very next night, the Cardinals returned the favor when Ray Washburn no-hit the Giants in a 2–0 win.

**You Can Look It Up!** SAN FRANCISCO'S OFFICIAL WEBSITE: www.sfgiants.com

# THE
# WORLD SERIES

**Major League Baseball** exaggerates a little bit when it calls its annual championship the World Series. After all, teams from only two countries can take part. But even as baseball grows in popularity around the globe, the World Series remains the top of the baseball heap. In this chapter, we'll dive into the championship-dogpile-on-the-mound that is World Series history, before taking a quick spin around the world to look at the international game. Earth is, after all, shaped just like a baseball.

## INSIDE:

*The New York Yankees won it all—again!—in 2009.*

# BEFORE
# THE WORLD SERIES

Pro baseball has been around since 1869, and the first league was organized just two years later. (See page 14.) Even before the birth of the World Series in 1903, the early pro leagues occasionally played against each other. But since the National League was so dominant, these championship series were mostly ignored by fans. The 1884 final between Providence of the NL and the Metropolitans of the American Association was attended by only a "few hundred spectators." In an end-of-season series in 1890, the tie-breaking Game 7 sold just 300 tickets and was canceled! But for you real baseball trivia nuts, here's a list of the pre-World Series "world" champs.

## "World's Series"
Played between the NL and AA

**1884**  Providence Grays (NL)

**1885**  Chicago White Stockings (NL)

**1886**  St. Louis Browns (AA)

**1887**  Detroit Wolverines (NL)

**1888**  New York Giants (NL)

**1889**  New York Giants (NL)

## Temple Cup
Played between the NL's first- and second-place teams

**1894**  New York Giants

**1895**  Cleveland Spiders

**1896**  Baltimore Orioles

# THE FIRST
# WORLD SERIES

With the AL two years old in 1903, its team owners wanted a shot at the older NL in a postseason championship series. NL owners were very reluctant, because, after all . . . what would happen if the upstart younger league won?! But the owners were also smart (and/or greedy), and they knew that such a series would draw huge crowds. So in 1903, the leagues agreed that their champions would meet after the regular season to determine a "World's" champion. Here are some fun firsts from that original World Series.

### First Champion:
Boston Pilgrims (AL) defeated the Pittsburg Pirates (NL) 5 games to 3

Note: The Pilgrims later became the Red Sox, and the Pirates' home city was spelled without the "h" back then.

### First World Series Home Run:
Jimmy Sebring of the Pirates in Game 1

### First World Series Strikeout:
Ed Phelps of Pittsburg by Boston's Cy Young in Game 1

### First World Series Stolen Base:
Honus Wagner of the Pirates in Game 1

### First Winning Pitcher (and Losing Pitcher):
Deacon Phillippe of Pittsburg beat Cy Young of Boston

### P.S.: The Second World Series
Remember how the NL didn't like the AL? No one disliked them more than New York Giants manager John McGraw. In 1904, McGraw's team won the NL—and then refused to play in the new World Series! So that meant that the second World Series wasn't played until two years after the first. In 1905, McGraw's Giants beat the AL's Philadelphia Athletics four games to one.

# EARLY SERIES HEROES

Some of baseball's most legendary figures earned their fame by shining during the World Series. When the gigantic spotlight of the sports world was on them, and when their teams needed them most, they came through.

MATHEWSON, N. Y. NAT'L

### ◀◀◀CHRISTY MATHEWSON, 1905

Perhaps the greatest World Series pitching performance came in the second Series. Mathewson threw three shutouts in six days, striking out 18 while walking only one! His New York Giants won their first title, beating the Philadelphia Athletics in five games.

### BABE RUTH, 1923

The great Bambino hit the first three of his 15 career World Series homers as the Yankees won their first title in the first year in their new home, Yankee Stadium. No wonder it would come to be known as "The House That Ruth Built."

### PEPPER MARTIN, 1934

The man they called the "Wild Horse of the Osage" set a Series record with 12 hits, batting .545 and helping the Cardinals beat the Athletics.

### DUKE SNIDER, 1955

The "Duke of Flatbush" was named for a neighborhood in Brooklyn, New York, where the Dodgers played. He blasted four homers with seven RBIs to lead the Dodgers to their first World Series triumph.

### LEW BURDETTE, 1957

The Milwaukee Braves right-hander won three games against the mighty New York Yankees, posting a 0.67 ERA.

### BILL MAZEROSKI, 1960

The Pirates second baseman became the first player to end a World Series with a home run, breaking a 9–9 tie in the bottom of the ninth of Game 7.

### ROBERTO CLEMENTE, 1971

Another Pirates hero, Clemente led Pittsburgh to the title by batting .414 with 12 hits. Sadly, he died the following year in a plane crash while delivering earthquake relief supplies to Nicaragua.

# THE BLACK SOX

The 1919 World Series will go down as one of baseball's darkest events. Some members of the White Sox took money from gangsters in return for "throwing" games–losing them on purpose. Exactly what each of the eight players accused of this baseball crime did to "earn" their money continues to be debated. But one thing is clear: The White Sox should have beaten the Cincinnati Reds, but they lost the World Series.

A year later, a court found the Sox players not guilty. Still, they were kicked out of baseball for life by Commissioner Kenesaw Mountain Landis. Among them was "Shoeless" Joe Jackson (right), whose .356 career batting average is still the third-highest ever.

# THE MIGHTY

As a lifelong fan of the Boston Red Sox, your humble author has to really restrain himself to write these pages and state this fact: In the history of American sports, no team has been as successful as the (gasp!) New York Yankees. The Bronx Bombers have won an incredible 27 World Series. (See the box on the opposite page to compare them to other North American sports teams.) Here are some stories and facts about the Yankees' amazing century of baseball success.

## First World Series Title

**1923** The Yankees moved into Yankee Stadium–the "House that Ruth Built"–this season and brought home their first championship. Babe Ruth hit three homers as the Yanks beat the New York Giants.

## First Back-to-Back Sweeps

**1927 & 1928** The Yanks romped in eight straight over the Pirates and Cardinals. After watching batting practice before the 1927 Series, one writer said about the Pirates, "If they ain't scared, they ain't human."

## All-Time Champs

**1936** With their fifth World Series title, the Yanks moved into the lead for the most championships by a franchise. They passed the Boston Red Sox, who had four at the time. No one has come close to catching the Bronx Bombers since.

# YANKEES

## First Team to Win Three in a Row . . . and More

**1938** Four teams had won back-to-back World Series, but none had gotten three until the Yanks won their third straight in 1938. They topped themselves by making it four in a row in 1939. Then in 1949–1953, they moved the record to five consecutive championships. Since then, only the 1972–1974 Oakland A's and, yes, the Yankees from 1998–2000 have even gotten to three.

## Subway Series

**2000** The Yankees capped off their third "threepeat" by defeating their crosstown rivals, the New York Mets, in what was called the Subway Series. Although every game was decided by one or two runs, the Yankees won in five. It was the Bombers' fourth title in five years.

## The Somewhat-Mighty Cardinals

If the Yankees are first, someone has to be second. With their championship in 2006, the St. Louis Cardinals secured that spot. The Cards have won ten World Series titles, along with 17 NL pennants. They've won in the 1920s, 1930s, 1940s, 1960s, and 2000s. They're first, of course, among NL teams.

## YANKEES VS. THE OTHERS

| TEAM | SPORT | NO. OF TITLES |
|------|-------|---------------|
| New York Yankees | Baseball | 27 |
| Montreal Canadiens | Hockey | 24 |
| Boston Celtics | Basketball | 17 |
| Green Bay Packers | Football | 12 |
| Pittsburgh Steelers | Football | 6* |

*The Steelers have won the most Super Bowls. The Packers earned nine of their NFL titles before the first Super Bowl was played in 1966.

# WORLD SERIES MVPS

Since 1955, a Most Valuable Player (or players, in some cases) has been chosen for each World Series. The award has gone to the winning team in every Series except one: 1960, when the Yankees' Bobby Richardson got a consolation prize after his team lost to the Pirates.

| | |
|---|---|
| 2009 | **Hideki MATSUI**, Yankees |
| 2008 | **Cole HAMELS**, Phillies |
| 2007 | **Mike LOWELL**, Red Sox |
| 2006 | **David ECKSTEIN**, Cardinals |
| 2005 | **Jermaine DYE**, White Sox |
| 2004 | **Manny RAMIREZ**, Red Sox |
| 2003 | **Josh BECKETT**, Marlins |
| 2002 | **Troy GLAUS**, Angels |
| 2001 | **Curt SCHILLING** and **Randy JOHNSON**, Diamondbacks |
| 2000 | **Derek JETER**, Yankees |
| 1999 | **Mariano RIVERA**, Yankees |
| 1998 | **Scott BROSIUS**, Yankees |
| 1997 | **Livan HERNANDEZ**, Marlins |
| 1996 | **John WETTELAND**, Yankees |
| 1995 | **Tom GLAVINE**, Braves |
| 1994 | Series cancelled. |
| 1993 | **Paul MOLITOR**, Blue Jays |
| 1992 | **Pat BORDERS**, Blue Jays |
| 1991 | **Jack MORRIS**, Twins |
| 1990 | **Jose RIJO**, Reds |
| 1989 | **Dave STEWART**, Athletics |
| 1988 | **Orel HERSHISER**, Dodgers |
| 1987 | **Frank VIOLA**, Twins |
| 1986 | **Ray KNIGHT**, Mets |
| 1985 | **Bret SABERHAGEN**, Royals |
| 1984 | **Alan TRAMMELL**, Tigers |
| 1983 | **Rick DEMPSEY**, Orioles |
| 1982 | **Darrell PORTER**, Cardinals |
| 1981 | **Ron CEY**, **Pedro GUERRERO**, and **Steve YEAGER**, Dodgers |
| 1980 | **Mike SCHMIDT**, Phillies |
| 1979 | **Willie STARGELL**, Pirates |

| 1978 | **Bucky DENT**, Yankees |
| 1977 | **Reggie JACKSON**, Yankees |
| 1976 | **Johnny BENCH**, Reds |
| 1975 | **Pete ROSE**, Reds |
| 1974 | **Rollie FINGERS**, Athletics |
| 1973 | **Reggie JACKSON**, Athletics |
| 1972 | **Gene TENACE**, Athletics |
| 1971 | **Roberto CLEMENTE**, Pirates |
| 1970 | **Brooks ROBINSON**, Orioles |
| 1969 | **Donn CLENDENON**, Mets |
| 1968 | **Mickey LOLICH**, Tigers |
| 1967 | **Bob GIBSON**, Cardinals |
| 1966 | **Frank ROBINSON**, Orioles |
| 1965 | **Sandy KOUFAX**, Dodgers |
| 1964 | **Bob GIBSON**, Cardinals |
| 1963 | **Sandy KOUFAX**, Dodgers |
| 1962 | **Ralph TERRY**, Yankees |
| 1961 | **Whitey FORD**, Yankees |
| 1960 | **Bobby RICHARDSON**, Yankees |
| 1959 | **Larry SHERRY**, Dodgers |
| 1958 | **Bob TURLEY**, Yankees |
| 1957 | **Lew BURDETTE**, Milwaukee |
| 1956 | **Don LARSEN**, Yankees |
| 1955 | **Johnny PODRES**, Dodgers |

# HERO TIME

## MR. OCTOBER

Reggie Jackson is one of only three players (and the only non-pitcher) to win more than one World Series MVP award, and the only one to do so with different teams. He got his first with Oakland by batting .310 with six RBIs in 1973. In 1977, however, he earned his nickname of "Mr. October" (the World Series is usually played in that month) with his clutch hitting. His peak performance–and one of the greatest ever–came in Game 6 vs. the Dodgers. He saw three pitches and hit three home runs. He ended with a total of five homers in the six games. It was a stunning display of power that made Jackson a legend.

# WORLD SERIES WINNERS

| YEAR | WINNER |
|------|--------|
| 2009 | New York **Yankees** |
| 2008 | Philadelphia **Phillies** |
| 2007 | Boston **Red Sox** |
| 2006 | St. Louis **Cardinals** |
| 2005 | Chicago **White Sox** |
| 2004 | Boston **Red Sox** |
| 2003 | Florida **Marlins** |
| 2002 | Anaheim **Angels** |
| 2001 | AZ **Diamondbacks** |
| 2000 | New York **Yankees** |
| 1999 | New York **Yankees** |
| 1998 | New York **Yankees** |
| 1997 | Florida **Marlins** |
| 1996 | New York **Yankees** |
| 1995 | Atlanta **Braves** |
| 1994 | Series cancelled. |
| 1993 | Toronto **Blue Jays** |
| 1992 | Toronto **Blue Jays** |
| 1991 | Minnesota **Twins** |
| 1990 | Cincinnati **Reds** |
| 1989 | Oakland **Athletics** |
| 1988 | Los Angeles **Dodgers** |
| 1987 | Minnesota **Twins** |
| 1986 | New York **Mets** |
| 1985 | Kansas City **Royals** |

| YEAR | WINNER |
|------|--------|
| 1984 | Detroit **Tigers** |
| 1983 | Baltimore **Orioles** |
| 1982 | St. Louis **Cardinals** |
| 1981 | Los Angeles **Dodgers** |
| 1980 | Philadelphia **Phillies** |
| 1979 | Pittsburgh **Pirates** |
| 1978 | New York **Yankees** |
| 1977 | New York **Yankees** |
| 1976 | Cincinnati **Reds** |
| 1975 | Cincinnati **Reds** |
| 1974 | Oakland **Athletics** |
| 1973 | Oakland **Athletics** |
| 1972 | Oakland **Athletics** |
| 1971 | Pittsburgh **Pirates** |
| 1970 | Baltimore **Orioles** |
| 1969 | New York **Mets** |
| 1968 | Detroit **Tigers** |
| 1967 | St. Louis **Cardinals** |
| 1966 | Baltimore **Orioles** |
| 1965 | Los Angeles **Dodgers** |
| 1964 | St. Louis **Cardinals** |
| 1963 | Los Angeles **Dodgers** |
| 1962 | New York **Yankees** |
| 1961 | New York **Yankees** |
| 1960 | Pittsburgh **Pirates** |

| YEAR | WINNER | YEAR | WINNER |
|------|--------|------|--------|
| 1959 | Los Angeles **Dodgers** | 1930 | Philadelphia **Athletics** |
| 1958 | New York **Yankees** | 1929 | Philadelphia **Athletics** |
| 1957 | Milwaukee **Braves** | 1928 | New York **Yankees** |
| 1956 | New York **Yankees** | 1927 | New York **Yankees** |
| 1955 | Brooklyn **Dodgers** | 1926 | St. Louis **Cardinals** |
| 1954 | New York **Giants** | 1925 | Pittsburgh **Pirates** |
| 1953 | New York **Yankees** | 1924 | Washington **Senators** |
| 1952 | New York **Yankees** | 1923 | New York **Yankees** |
| 1951 | New York **Yankees** | 1922 | New York **Giants** |
| 1950 | New York **Yankees** | 1921 | New York **Giants** |
| 1949 | New York **Yankees** | 1920 | Cleveland **Indians** |
| 1948 | Cleveland **Indians** | 1919 | Cincinnati **Reds** |
| 1947 | New York **Yankees** | 1918 | Boston **Red Sox** |
| 1946 | St. Louis **Cardinals** | 1917 | Chicago **White Sox** |
| 1945 | Detroit **Tigers** | 1916 | Boston **Red Sox** |
| 1944 | St. Louis **Cardinals** | 1915 | Boston **Red Sox** |
| 1943 | New York **Yankees** | 1914 | Boston **Braves** |
| 1942 | St. Louis **Cardinals** | 1913 | Philadelphia **Athletics** |
| 1941 | New York **Yankees** | 1912 | Boston **Red Sox** |
| 1940 | Cincinnati **Reds** | 1911 | Philadelphia **Athletics** |
| 1939 | New York **Yankees** | 1910 | Philadelphia **Athletics** |
| 1938 | New York **Yankees** | 1909 | Pittsburgh **Pirates** |
| 1937 | New York **Yankees** | 1908 | Chicago **Cubs** |
| 1936 | New York **Yankees** | 1907 | Chicago **Cubs** |
| 1935 | Detroit **Tigers** | 1906 | Chicago **White Sox** |
| 1934 | St. Louis **Cardinals** | 1905 | New York **Giants** |
| 1933 | New York **Giants** | 1904 | No Series held. |
| 1932 | New York **Yankees** | 1903 | Boston **Red Sox** |
| 1931 | St. Louis **Cardinals** | | |

# WORLD OF

Baseball started in the cities and fields of the United States, but it quickly spread to other countries near and far. Today, it's played in more countries than ever before, and players from more than a dozen countries have found homes in the big leagues. Here's a quick rundown on some important events in world baseball history.

**1873** A schoolteacher from the U.S. brought baseball to Japan.

**1878** Cuba formed the first baseball league outside the U.S.

◀◀◀**1888** Superstar pitcher Al Spalding (yes, he later founded the sporting-goods company) led a world tour of star players. After touring Europe, they played in Egypt (near the Sphinx!) and in Australia.

**1927** The first American pro players visited Japan on an exhibition tour . . . but they were not major leaguers. They were from the Eastern Colored League, a league of African Americans.

**1931** Lou Gehrig, Lefty Grove, and other major league stars toured Japan four years later. It would be the first of many similar trips. One tour in 1934 included Babe Ruth.

**1946** A millionaire named Jorge Pasquel dangled big money in front of some big leaguers to get them to join his team in the Mexican League. More than 20 accepted, but they played there only briefly.

**1949** Minnie Minoso joined the Cleveland Indians. He was the first black Latino player in the big leagues. Earlier, some light-skinned Cubans had played.

**1957** A team from Monterrey, Mexico, won the Little League World Series. They were the first team from outside the U.S. to win the title.

# BASEBALL

**1964** Masanori Murakami pitched for the San Francisco Giants, making him the first Japanese-born player in the bigs. He stayed for two seasons.

**1969** The Montreal Expos were added to the NL; they were the first Canadian team in the majors.

**1984** At the Summer Olympics in Los Angeles, baseball was played as a demonstration sport; that is, no medals were officially awarded in the competition, which was won by Japan. (For more, see page 150.)

**1989** The Australian Baseball League was born.

**1992** Baseball was made an official medal sport in the Summer Olympics.

**1994** Pitcher Chan Ho Park was signed by the LA Dodgers. Park was the first Korean player in the majors.

**1999** The Cuban national team and the Baltimore Orioles played a historic set of games, one in Havana and one in Baltimore.

**2000** The Major League Baseball season opened with a two-game series between the Cubs and the Mets in Tokyo, Japan.

**2006** For the first time, national teams fielding major league players faced off in an international championship. Japan won the World Baseball Classic by defeating Cuba in the final. The Japanese won the WBC again in 2009.

## MLB PLAYERS FROM AROUND THE GLOBE

As of Opening Day 2009, players from these nations and territories were on major league teams.

| COUNTRY | NO. OF PLAYERS |
|---|---|
| Aruba | 1 |
| Australia | 2 |
| Canada | 15 |
| Colombia | 6 |
| Curaçao | 1 |
| Dominican Republic | 91 |
| Japan | 12 |
| Mexico | 18 |
| Nicaragua | 1 |
| Panama | 6 |
| Puerto Rico | 34 |
| South Korea | 5 |
| Taiwan | 1 |
| Venezuela | 46 |
| Virgin Islands | 1 |

# BASEBALL IN THE
# OLYMPICS

This story has a sad ending . . . for now. In 1992, baseball was made a medal sport in the Summer Olympics. But because the Summer Olympics are held during the MLB season, the top players never took part. The U.S. team, for example, was made up of college and minor league players.

Baseball actually had a lot longer history at the Olympics. At six prior Games, baseball was played as a "demonstration" sport. Winning players were not awarded Olympic medals, since the games were played merely as a showcase for the sport. The first was in 1912 in Stockholm, Sweden.

Cuba (see chart below) took home the most gold medals after baseball became an official Olympic sport in 1992. Women's fast-pitch softball was added in 1996, and U.S. teams dominated, winning gold in 1996, 2000, and 2004. They were upset by Japan in 2008.

Now here's the bad news. The Olympic Committee voted to kick baseball and softball out of the Olympics, beginning in 2012. Booo!

## Olympic Baseball Results

| YEAR | GOLD | SILVER | BRONZE |
| --- | --- | --- | --- |
| 1992 | Cuba | Taiwan | Japan |
| 1996 | Cuba | Japan | United States |
| 2000 | United States | Cuba | South Korea |
| 2004 | Cuba | Australia | Japan |
| 2008 | South Korea | Cuba | United States |

## Olympic Softball Results

| YEAR | GOLD | SILVER | BRONZE |
| --- | --- | --- | --- |
| 1996 | United States | China | Australia |
| 2000 | United States | Japan | Australia |
| 2004 | United States | Australia | Japan |
| 2008 | Japan | United States | Australia |

# WORLD BASEBALL CLASSIC

Looking for a way to let the best players in the world play for their countries, Major League Baseball came up with the World Baseball Classic. It's now been held twice, and each time it was a huge success. The games are played during spring training so that superstars from all countries can play. Dozens of major leaguers trade their team uniforms for their countries' colors. Here's a quick look at the first two WBCs. The next is scheduled for 2013.

**2006** With early-round games in Japan, Puerto Rico, Arizona, and Florida, this was truly an international tournament. The U.S. was eliminated in the second round. A strong Dominican team was knocked out in the semifinals by Cuba, a longtime international powerhouse. In the other semifinal, Japan beat Korea 6-0. That was a bit of a surprise since Korea had already beaten Japan twice in earlier rounds. In the final game, Daisuke Matsuzaka of the Red Sox helped earn his MVP trophy by silencing the Cuban bats. "Dice-K" finished the tournament with three wins and a tiny 1.38 ERA.

**2009** The U.S. had a very strong team—including stars such as Roy Oswalt, Jake Peavy, Derek Jeter, Jimmy Rollins, David Wright, and Ryan Braun—and high hopes for a better result. However, Japan knocked off the U.S. in a semifinal game behind the pitching of ace Matsuzaka. In the other semifinal, Korea surprised many by defeating Cuba. In the all-Asian final, Ichiro Suzuki (right) of the Mariners stroked a game-winning single in the tenth inning to lead Japan to victory over its archrival Korea before a packed house at Dodger Stadium. Matsuzaka was again the MVP of the WBC.

# BASEBALL
# BASICS

If you've gotten this far, you probably know the basic rules of baseball. Still, it's always nice to have them all in one place for easy reference. So here are some of the standard rules for America's National Pastime.

* Nine players take the field for the team that is on defense.

* The team at bat cycles through the nine players in its batting order.

* The batting team continues to bat until it makes three outs.

* A batted ball that is caught before it hits the ground is an out.

* On a force play, the fielder with the ball can make an out by tagging the base before the oncoming runner reaches it.

* On a tag play, the fielder must touch the baserunner with the ball (or with his glove holding the ball) before the runner reaches the base.

* A run is scored when a baserunner touches home plate after having touched the other three bases in order.

* The pitcher starts each play by throwing the ball toward home plate.

* A pitch that goes through the strike zone (over home plate, from armpits to knees) is a strike. A pitch that misses that zone is a ball.

* If a batter swings and misses at a pitch, it's a strike even if the pitch missed the strike zone.

* A ball hit outside the white foul lines is a foul ball. The first two foul balls count as strikes. Note: A batter can't strike out by hitting a foul ball unless he or she bunts it.

* In the big leagues, the minors, and in college, games are complete after nine innings. The number of innings can differ at other levels, such as six innings for Little League.

We could go on and on, of course, but those are the basics.

# THE INFIELD FLY RULE

Baseball's rules are, for the most part, fairly easy to understand. But one rule that always causes a lot of confusion is the infield fly rule. Once you "get it," it's easy to understand. But sometimes it takes a while to do that. So here's our take on it.

## The Rule:

On a fly ball hit above the infield, the umpire may declare the batter out even while the ball is in the air.

## When It Can Happen:

When there are runners on first and second and there are fewer than two outs.

## Why It Can Happen:

Without this rule, an infielder could drop an infield fly on purpose. A baserunner won't try to advance when the ball is in the air because he expects the fly ball to be caught—if he ran, the infielder could throw to the base he left and force him out for a double play. But if the runner stayed on base, the infielder could let the ball drop, pick it up, and then throw to the next base for a force out.

## Why, Part II:

The rule was put in place in 1895 after wily fielders started dropping infield flies and forcing out multiple baserunners for double and triple plays.

## What to Look for:

On an infield pop, watch the home-plate ump, who will raise his arm in the air and call the batter out. He might wait to see whether the ball drifts to the outfield before making the call.

# BASEBALL RULES
# QUIZ!

Time to put on your baseball thinking caps and test your knowledge of these baseball rules. The answers to these seamhead-teasers are at the bottom. Remember, three strikes and you're out!

**1** A ball is hit toward the outfield fence. It hits the ground and bounces over the fence. What's the call?

**2** A ground ball hits a baserunner moving between first and second base. What's the call?

**3** A fielder chasing after a ball rolling in the outfield throws his glove at the ball to stop it. What's the ruling?

**4** A hard ground ball is snagged by the pitcher. But the ball gets stuck in his glove. What can he do?

**5** A runner from first runs headfirst into the shortstop, who is covering second in an attempt to help turn a double play. The shortstop is knocked over. What does the umpire do?

**6** On a fly ball caught in the outfield, a runner tags up and scores. But he leaves third base too early. What should the defense do?

**7** The catcher is circling under a high foul pop. He tosses away his mask so he won't step on it, but he trips over a bat lying in the opponents' on-deck circle and misses the ball. Is the batter out?

ANSWERS: 1. Ground-rule double. 2. The runner is out and the play is over. 3. The batter gets an automatic triple. 4. If he can't pull the ball out in time, he can throw the entire ball-and-glove combo to first base. 5. He calls both the baserunner and the batter out for interference. 6. An infielder with the ball should go touch third base and appeal to an umpire, who should call the runner out. 7. No, the catcher just had bad luck, but the umpire might warn both teams to keep the on-deck area clear.

# FIND OUT MORE

More books have been written about baseball than about almost any other sport. No matter what area of baseball you are interested in, you'll find a fiction or nonfiction book that meets your needs. Here are only a tiny handful of the thousands of great baseball books.

## BOOKS

### EYEWITNESS: BASEBALL
By James Buckley, Jr. (yes . . . me!)
(DK, 2010)
*Tons of photos from throughout baseball history, plus sections on the minors, the Negro Leagues, the World Series, and more.*

### PLAY BALL!
*The Official Major League Guide for Young Players*
By James Buckley, Jr.
(DK, 2002)
*Step-by-step photos are mixed with tips from major leaguers to help any young superstar improve his or her game!*

### SHOELESS JOE AND ME
By Bill Gutman
(HarperCollins, 2003)
*This is one of a series of novels in which a young fan is sent back in time to meet and help a baseball hero from the past. In this book, it's Shoeless Joe Jackson.*

### WE ARE THE SHIP
By Kadir Nelson
(Jump at the Sun/Hyperion, 2008)
*Stunning paintings illustrate this award-winning history of the Negro Leagues. Meet Josh Gibson, Satchel Paige, and other heroes.*

## WEBSITES

**www.mlb.com**
*Every team, every player, every game. The official site of Major League Baseball includes video, articles, stats, and history. It's a baseball fan's dream site!*

**www.baseball-reference.com**
*Stat heads, rejoice! This numbers-packed site can help baseball fanatics find out just about anything about just about any player, from where they were born to how many hits they had to how much they got paid.*

**www.littleleague.org**
*The world's biggest youth baseball organization has a site that includes news from national championships, a trivia game, tips on playing, and info about Little League history.*

# GLOSSARY

**ballot box**   a box used to collect votes before they are counted

**banned**   kicked out, prevented from participating

**bigoted**   believing something negative without having a good reason, often used when talking about race

**expansion team**   a new franchise added to a pro sports league

**intentional**   by choice, on purpose

**lathe**   a machine on which wood is carved as it spins very, very fast

**pennant**   an American League or National League championship, or the flag that's awarded to a league champion

**performance-enhancing**   giving a person the ability to perform a job better. This term is often used to describe illegal substances taken by some athletes.

**prototypical**   a perfect example of something

**Soviet Union**   a very large state made up of Russia and a dozen or so smaller nations. The Soviet Union existed from 1922 until 1991.

**stained**   in this case, covered with a paint or chemical

**translate**   to express in one language the sense of words or text in another language

# INDEX

# IT'S OVER!

We'll wrap up our extensive look at baseball with some thoughts from one of the game's greatest philosophers. Yogi Berra was a three-time MVP as a catcher and outfielder for the Yankees from 1946–1963. The Hall of Famer holds numerous World Series records, including games played, hits, and runs. He's celebrated for his great play, but he's also famous for the very odd things he says. In fact, one of his books is subtitled "I Really Didn't Say Everything I Said!" So let's end with a few of his most inexplicable gems.

(Someone asked him what time it was.) *"You mean now?"* he asked.

*"When you come to a fork in the road . . . take it!"*

*"If the world were perfect, it wouldn't be."*

*"I usually take a two-hour nap from one to four."*

*"It gets late early out here."*

*"You can observe a lot by watching."*

*"It ain't over 'til it's over."*